KT-155-433

CRISIS IN THE CLASSROOM

crisis
in the
classroom

The Exam Debacle and the Way Ahead
for Scottish Education

Lindsay Paterson

MAINSTREAM
PUBLISHING

EDINBURGH AND LONDON

Copyright © Lindsay Paterson, 2000
All rights reserved
The moral right of the author has been asserted

First published in Great Britain in 2000 by
MAINSTREAM PUBLISHING COMPANY (EDINBURGH) LTD
7 Albany Street
Edinburgh EH1 3UG

ISBN 1 84018 420 5

No part of this book may be reproduced or transmitted in any
form or by any means without written permission from the
publisher, except by a reviewer who wishes to quote brief
passages in connection with a review written for insertion in a
newspaper, magazine or broadcast

A catalogue record for this book is available
from the British Library

Typeset in 10.5 on 13pt Apollo MT
Printed and bound in Great Britian
by Cox and Wyman Ltd

CONTENTS

Preface

The exams crisis of the summer of 2000 was, first of all, a traumatic experience for thousands of students. But it was more than that. It brought into sharp focus some fundamental questions about the character and quality of Scottish education. Aiming to provide 'opportunity for all', the new Higher Still examination system was meant to be the latest phase in the development of Scotland's comprehensive secondary schools. It was supposed to provide equal opportunities for everyone in school and college in their late teenage years, while also maintaining high academic standards.

The chaos which surrounded the issuing of the results did not only bring into question the competence of the body which administers them. It also brought back to the surface some deep concerns about the entire reform and about the role of examinations in young people's education. Are we subjecting our students to too much assessment? Are the cultural and human purposes of education being lost in a welter of testing? Is the laudable aim of providing wide opportunity leading to a dilution of the quality of what is on offer?

The events also provided an early test of the new Scottish parliament. Its inquiries began to probe the role of the country's civic institutions. Maybe, some people began to surmise, the civic identity that had sustained Scotland for so long was in need of drastic renovation. Perhaps the crisis had come about because of complacency – because the people in charge of Scotland's civic life are not truly accountable. Maybe more attention should have been paid to the warnings of teachers and others over the years that the new system was flawed.

This book deals with these issues – not only with the immediate events of summer 2000, but also with the wider questions about Scottish education, Scottish culture and Scottish politics. It is in eight chapters. The first recounts the story of the chaotic events of August 2000. The next two then set these in a historical context: Chapter 2 traces the Highers for the century following their founding in 1888, and Chapter 3 looks at why a consensus emerged in the late 1980s that they needed to be reformed. Chapter 4 traces the development of the reform that did emerge – Higher Still, from its announcement in 1994 until the first group of students sat the new exams in summer 2000. Chapter 5 outlines the political context that helped to decide what happened next – the context of the Scottish parliament around which had grown enormous hopes for its ability to renew Scottish society and Scottish institutions. Chapter 6 analyses the evidence presented to the inquiries which the parliament set up. And Chapters 7 and 8 draw conclusions – for Scottish education and for how policy is made. There is then a guide to further reading, which also indicates the sources on which this book draws.

ACKNOWLEDGEMENTS

Crisis in the Classroom has benefited from advice and information that has kindly been supplied by several people in Scottish education. My thanks go in particular to Ken Macdonald of BBC Scotland and to David McCrone of Edinburgh University. I am also grateful for suggestions and for material that would not otherwise have been in the public domain from John Aberdein, Alice Brown, Jack Carr, Tom Conlon, Gordon Lawrie, Tony McManus, Raymond Robertson, Liz Walker, the staff at the Scottish Parliament Information Centre, and several other teachers and lecturers who preferred to remain anonymous.

CHAPTER I

Anatomy of a Disaster: August 2000

August 2000 is not a month that the school students of Scotland will want to remember. Waiting for examination results is stressful enough at the best of times. You've worked hard all year, you've gone through the anxiety of sitting the exams, and then you've had to put it out of your mind for three months while the markers and checkers and computers put the results together. And then the brown envelope arrives on your doormat some morning in mid-August. This ritual has been going on now in Scotland for over a century. So when it fails, in any way, people feel let down, disappointed, angry and cynical.

The Highers are at the heart of the exam system, and symbolise Scottish education as a whole. Ever since they were founded in 1888, they have embodied the academic standards to which Scottish education as a whole has aspired, even in the days when they were taken by only a tiny minority of students. Massive educational expansion in the last few decades, encouraged by Scotland's successful system of comprehensive secondary schools, has brought the Highers within the grasp of nearly a half of all students, encouraged since the late 1980s by the generally successful new Standard Grade exams. The Higher Still reform was meant to extend this opportunity further, by providing new exams just below the Higher level that would cater for nearly all students in fifth and sixth year of school and equivalent stages in college. So the chaos surrounding the first year of the new system affected a very large number of people indeed – not just the eighty thousand or so candidates who sat the new exams, but also their parents, relatives and friends, and the hundreds of thousands of students expecting to embark on their first Highers year in the autumn of 2000. What happened in August 2000 was a truly national calamity.

'WE ARE LOOKING INTO THE INTEGRITY OF ALL OUR RESULTS'

The first inkling in public that something was about to go badly wrong came on BBC Radio Scotland on 8 August. The results were due to be issued two days later, and it is normal practice for them to be sent to the universities first, so that they are able to take decisions about whether students have achieved high enough grades to get in, and so as to allow them to be in a position to answer students' questions. But, on 8 August, the Universities and Colleges Admissions Service (UCAS) announced that it had received nothing from the body which runs the exams, the Scottish Qualifications Authority. Students would have to wait to hear what their fate was.

The following day, things were beginning to gather momentum. Still before any results had been issued, Sam Galbraith, the minister in the Education Department of the Scottish government, had announced that he was taking over the SQA's own 'independent' inquiry into what was going on. The SQA was warning that some students would not get their results on time either, although it said this would affect only a few thousand people.

So when results day came, Thursday, 10 August, the normal stress of the occasion was already being made worse. There was already a sense of impending crisis, although the scale of it was not yet fully apparent.

Here's how Radio Scotland's education correspondent, Ken Macdonald, reported the story on *Good Morning Scotland* that day: 'It should have been the bright dawn of a new system of qualifications – the first of its kind in the world. Alongside the existing Highers, new grades at intermediate and access levels. And new subjects to link the classroom with the workplace, from civil engineering to philosophy. But that's not quite how it has turned out: the new computer system needed to collect the results has been plagued with problems. More than a thousand candidates will find their exam certificates are incomplete. And there's been a delay in getting the exam results to universities, with institutions warning that some pupils may have to wait until next week before they know if they've got a place. The Scottish Qualifications Authority is now facing an independent inquiry into the problems, ordered by education minister Sam Galbraith. But for the 145,000 people who've been waiting for their envelopes, that's not important right now. They just want to know how they've done.'

Some were to have a long wait, because matters started to deteriorate very rapidly from that day onwards. Many envelopes did not arrive. Students phoned their schools (as they had been told to do by the SQA) and found that the schools hadn't received the results either.

The frustration was put forcefully by one student in an email to the BBC website: 'None of my friends has received results from Higher or Standard Grade exams. [The SQA has] refused to give results over the telephone. Post Office staff are pulling their hair out. We have been guinea pigs.'

But the real crisis erupted the following day. Schools started getting their results, and teachers were outraged at the extent of the inaccuracies. Their star students were recorded as having performed dismally. For example, *The Scotsman* reported on 16 August that the best student in the Higher physics class at Holy Rood High School in Edinburgh – a pupil who had never previously received a mark lower than an A – had apparently failed. Indeed, entire classes were reported by the SQA as having failed – almost the whole Higher computing class in George Watson's College in Edinburgh, and all the Higher English pupils at Portobello High School, both schools with excellent academic records. And students who were lucky to have scraped into a Higher course at all had received suspiciously good grades.

At first these stories were isolated, but, as the media started digging, the true awfulness of the situation became apparent. The BBC were flooded by calls to their Glasgow newsroom, and on Friday, 11 August, their website received a record number of emails. Even a BBC team which had been filming in Fochabers – planning for the routine reporting of the results – were approached by anxious students and parents asking them to take up their own cases.

One poignant case from elsewhere in Scotland that was aired by

Ken Macdonald involved a student who was on holiday in Spain. Her parents had rung the SQA hotline and were told that she had received an A in all her subjects. When the girl phoned home, as she had previously arranged, she was naturally delighted. Next day the certificate arrived, and she had in fact received two As, two Bs and a C. But she was not contactable by phone, and thus remained oblivious to the true situation until her holiday was over. Another student told the *Daily Mail* on 12 August that he had been informed by the SQA that he had got an A, a B, a C and a fail, with one result missing. But his school had been told that he had three As, a B and a C. He described the confusion as 'institutionalised torture'.

The official line from the SQA and the minister was still that the media were exaggerating the story. But it had now run out of control. The principals of Scotland's universities had heard enough examples of apparently wrong or incomplete results to issue an ultimatum: on 11 August they gave the SQA 24 hours to sort things out. The SQA continued to deny that there were any mistakes (and its website continued to boast that all the certificates had been delivered, even though thousands of students were still waiting). But the officials in the Education Department were also hearing privately the same stories as the journalists were picking up. Just before BBC TV's *Reporting Scotland* went on air at 6.30 that evening, Sam Galbraith broke off his holiday in Stornoway to concede that some results were wrong. But he added that it would be irresponsible and ridiculous to cast doubt on all the certificates, a view that was shared the following morning by the general secretary of the largest teachers' union, the EIS, who told the *Daily Record* that 'it would be adding insult to injury to youngsters to imply you cannot have belief in the bits of paper you have got'.

The problem by then, however, was deciding which bits of paper could be believed. Although the SQA was still convinced that only a tiny fraction of the certificates were wrong, it could not say which. So no student could be sure that his or her own certificate was correct. So doubt was inevitably being cast on all of them, a point that had to be conceded by the SQA, when a spokeswoman told *The Scotsman* on 12 August that it was 'looking into the integrity of all the results'. Asked by journalist Andrew Denholm if she could guarantee the integrity of any result, she replied, 'No.'

CHIEF EXECUTIVE RESIGNS

Over the weekend of 12–13 August, the problems escalated. Early on the Saturday morning, the official position was still that matters were not serious because only a few certificates were affected. It was not necessary to check all results, and it was not necessary to suspend university admissions. It was also being denied that Ron Tuck, chief executive of the SQA, would resign. By mid-afternoon, however, he had done so. That exposed the minister, and calls for Sam Galbraith to resign were now being made by the SNP, the main opposition party in the Scottish parliament, and also – perhaps more tellingly in a political sense – by ordinary people interviewed by journalists. The Labour convener of the parliament's Education Committee, Mary Mulligan, proposed on Saturday morning that there should be a parliamentary inquiry into the mess.

On the Sunday morning, a summit took place involving the Scottish government, the university principals and the SQA at which a guarantee was given that all results would be rechecked by the following Thursday, and that in the meantime the university admissions process would be put on hold. This was inevitable, since an offer of a university place is a legally binding contract. But it now opened up a potential new problem for Scottish students. The A-level results in the rest of the UK were due to appear on Thursday; if Scottish students were still waiting for their results at that point, they could be at a disadvantage.

The examples of bewildered students were now mounting up. As Campbell Dickson, the headteacher of Nairn Academy, put it in the *Daily Record*, 'This is a human tragedy of enormous proportions.'

Here is one of dozens of stories that were emailed to the BBC. It comes from Laura McConnell: 'I was one of the people who failed to receive the dreaded brown envelope on Thursday and so decided to phone the SQA helpline to find out if I could get my results over the phone. I did and was elated when I found that I had an A in English, geography and physics, a B for maths and an incomplete music result which I presumed would be an A because it is my best subject. My joy lasted until this Saturday morning when I finally received my certificate only to discover that the only A I had been awarded was for English. I had Bs for physics and geography, and a C for maths – needless to say, I was a bit upset! I phoned to check with the SQA and was told that my certificate was correct. Meanwhile, I heard that a friend who had failed all his prelims had somehow been awarded four As and had only failed maths. I wouldn't grudge him his grades, but it did make me wonder how on earth I ended up with mine when I was predicted to get straight As.'

Teachers were also finding astonishing anomalies. *The Herald* reported that a student in Lochaber High School in Fort William was given an A pass in economics, even though she had not even sat the exam.

Other concerns started to emerge. One was over marking. In an email to the BBC, Gordon Rennet, head of the modern studies department at the High School of Dundee, raised questions about the quality of the way in which the marking of the exams was administered: 'The SQA found it almost impossible to raise markers for this year's diet of exams. This resulted in frenzied phone calls to departments pleading for potential markers in the last week of term. I have heard that retired teachers with no experience of the current syllabus were drafted in in an attempt to meet deadlines. I have a colleague who attempted to update a teacher who had been retired for ten years and was about to mark Higher history papers.'

Numerous markers were confirming this. One, David Cooney from Hamilton, a marker with 24 years' experience, wrote in *The Herald* on 16 August that the usual quality checks on markers had not been in place in 2000, and that he was so disillusioned that he would never mark again for the SQA.

The emerging official explanation of the mess was that it was due to data-processing problems in entering the results of internal assessment: that is, the results of tests which students sat during the year, which were meant to be marked by teachers and then sent on to the SQA. As we will see in Chapters 4 and 6, teachers had been complaining throughout the year that the SQA seemed to be incapable of processing this data correctly. In *The Herald* on 17 August, this explanation from the SQA was rejected as missing the point by Professor Christopher Johnson of the department of computer science at Glasgow University. Human beings are nearly always responsible, usually senior managers: 'If the computer system does not work as intended, that is a management failure. We have seen loads of well-publicised failures for almost twenty years now of computer systems to deliver the complete package of services they were intended to provide. I would have thought we had seen enough for the penny to have dropped by now. The key point is that in most cases of computer failure, the computer is doing exactly what it is being programmed to do. It is the human part which fails.'

Meanwhile, the SQA had appointed an interim chief executive, Bill Morton, who had previously worked with the then chairman of the SQA board, David Miller, at the Local Enterprise Company in Forth Valley. Leaks from inside the SQA depicted an organisation collapsing in panic over the summer, despite the public assurances. Mr Miller phoned me on 15 August to report that, on the day on which all certificates were meant to have been issued, he had seen thousands of them lying around at the SQA offices in Dalkeith. He also told me that he had been informed by a middle manager as far back as June that the highest level of accuracy that they could manage on the certificates was 80 per cent. (Mr Miller assured me that I could report this phone call in public, and could say it came from him.)

That level of error – 20 per cent – was still being fiercely denied. For example, the body representing the university principals claimed in *The Scotsman* on 17 August that at most 7 per cent of results were wrong. But a higher level seemed to be confirmed later in the same day by the universities' admissions service UCAS. Its deputy chief executive Anthony McLaren said that it had been told by the SQA that there were some 2,800 inaccurate results among the roughly 17,800 it had been given. That is 16 per cent. On 18 August David Miller announced the results of the SQA's checking: there were only 5 per cent inaccuracies. The inconsistency between it and the UCAS figure has never been explained. So incredible was the figure of 5 per cent that it became one of the main sources of the next problem: the avalanche of appeals against unexpectedly low grades.

Mr Miller's public statement also gave two other hostages to fortune. One concerned the 5,000 candidates whose certificates were wrong. He offered the unambiguous assurance that 'we have identified every one of these candidates by name and will be working to confirm their final result'. That was strictly correct, but probably gave a false sense of security – as if the next stage of the checking was straightforward. In fact, several of these candidates were still waiting for their results a week later. Marian Docherty, the headteacher of St Thomas of Aquin's High School in Edinburgh, reported to the *Evening News* on 24 August that there continued to be 'extraordinary' problems in English, maths and several other subjects. Kirsty Anderson, a student at St Augustine's High School in the city, was still waiting for her results in two subjects, as was Khadaji Shahid from the same school, who told the paper's reporter that her planned course at Stevenson College was still very uncertain: 'I can't confirm the Highers that I want to do because I don't even know if I have to resit any exams. I've been in touch with the school and I've spoken to people at the SQA, but there doesn't seem to be any-thing happening at all.' That bewilderment was still widespread across Scotland.

The other rather inexplicable assurance from Mr Miller's state-ment was that 'no grade for any Higher or Certificate of Sixth Year Studies candidate will be lowered'. This was defensible only if the SQA had already worked out exactly what had gone wrong, and had found that it was entirely due to some marks having gone missing. Any other source of error would have resulted in some results dropping as well as some rising – and, as was being reported, some people were getting grades that were surprisingly high. The suspicion was aroused that the decision not to lower results was essentially a political one. It was alleged that the SQA and the government could get away with this decision because the problems that it would cause would not be apparent for several years – not until the students with inaccurately high grades found difficulties in coping with the university courses onto which their inflated grades had allowed them to be admitted.

'NO ONE WILL MISS OUT ON A UNIVERSITY PLACE'
Sam Galbraith had insisted right from the beginning – on the BBC's *Reporting Scotland* on 11 August – that 'no one will miss out on a university place because of these problems'. This unequivocal statement became the subject of considerable refinement and interpretation over the following two weeks. To try to ensure that the spirit of it would be honoured, two universities actually gave up on the SQA on 17 August. Aberdeen and Napier announced that they would be accepting students on the basis of the predictions which their schools had made of their Highers performance. Paisley and Stirling followed a day later. Tony Higgins, the chief executive of the UK-wide universities' admissions service UCAS, could not share Mr Galbraith's optimism, pointing out the particular problems faced by students who had to enter the clearing system. Clearing is for people who fail to gain the grades required to win a place on their first-choice course, and so have to go into a pool of candidates competing for the left-over places elsewhere.

David Caldwell, chief executive of the organisation which represents the university principals, confirmed Mr Higgins's fears in *The Scotsman* on 17 August: 'The nature and tight timescale of the clearing process makes it difficult to give any absolute guarantee that no disadvantage will be suffered.'

The Scottish government's line was, by then, that students would have to be 'flexible' to avoid losing out. Mr Galbraith had issued no such caveat on 11 August, but the official explanation was that his statement had 'reflected what he was being told at the time, in a developing situation'.

In fact, probably very few students did lose out in clearing, since most other Scottish universities were being flexible too, and since very few Scottish students go into clearing for places at universities elsewhere in the UK. But what seemed undeniable was that many pupils endured yet more stress and bother in trying to confirm the places they thought they had won. They may not have lost out, but they certainly lost a lot of sleep. One student's experience illustrates this. She had a great deal of difficulty persuading the university to which she had applied that she really had gained a B in her Higher modern studies (I have given her a fictitious name because she requested anonymity):

- 10 August: no certificate arrives, so Fiona's mother phones the SQA helpline to be told that her daughter got a B in Higher modern studies, but that it has not been recorded on the certificate because the details of the internal assessments have not been received from her school.
- 11 August: certificate arrives, but with modern studies recorded at the end under 'incomplete courses'. A phone call to the SQA produces the assurance that things are being sorted out.
- 18 August: a letter arrives from the SQA saying that there are still problems, but giving no indication of what these are or when they will be resolved.
- 21 August: a radio announcement says that the SQA has checked all the certificates. A phone call to the authority finds that the modern studies result is still missing. Fiona's mother insists that the person who took the call gets her supervisor, who decides to ask the school to fax the details of the internal assessments again. Her mother also phones UCAS (because the university's own helpline is constantly engaged) to be told that it, too, has received the incorrect result. What's more, it is obliged to keep Fiona's place open only until 30 August.
- 22 August: a phone call finally gets through to the university, which says that, because it has not received confirmation that Fiona has done well enough in modern studies, it will be sending an official letter of rejection. The only consolation that can be offered is that she might get a place next year.
- 23 August: another phone call manages to persuade the accom-

modation officer at the university to hold open a place in a hall of residence for the time being, but it will be in Fiona's last choice of hall.

Fiona did eventually get into the university (although not into her preferred hall) and so she does not count as someone who has been disadvantaged by what was going on. But she and her family were put through enormous, unexpected and unnecessary stress.

In some respects, however, students like Fiona are not even the worst affected. Once they get into university, they will be able to put all this behind them. There is a more acute problem for people who left education altogether with the certificates of the year 2000, and for whom no later exam pass will supersede it. They will carry the doubts about that certificate's accuracy with them for the rest of their lives.

'YOU'RE FLUENT IN RUSSIAN AND YOU FAILED HIGHER RUSSIAN'

The climax of the public debate in August came on Tuesday 22nd, when the BBC organised a special programme at which Sam Galbraith and the SQA chief executive, Bill Morton, were interrogated by an audience of students, teachers, representatives of some other educational organisations, politicians and academics. The Education Department suggested that appearing on this programme was a 'brave' decision by the minister. Observers felt it was the least he could have done, especially since the BBC had threatened to go ahead regardless with or without his participation, and would have used a panel of people who would all have been critical of the government and the SQA.

The debate was chaired by the BBC journalist Anne Mackenzie. Near the beginning she turned to Sasha Voronov, a student from Boroughmuir High School in Edinburgh: 'Sasha, you're Russian. You sat Higher Russian. You failed Higher Russian. You're fluent in Russian.'

Sasha smiled diffidently and said he hoped it would be sorted out. Since his case had already been aired on Scottish Television, Mr Galbraith and Mr Morton were prepared with a technical explanation of what had gone wrong. But the indictment was inescapable. Here was an exam system that appeared to be so ridiculous that it could judge a native Russian speaker as incapable of speaking his own language.

It must have been quite an ordeal for Mr Morton and Mr Galbraith, because with one exception – a former board member of the SQA – every speaker was hostile. But it made riveting TV, and provoked another flood of emails to the BBC's website. The programme was a nice balance of students' experience, teachers' expertise and general points offering explanations. It was also neatly complemented by the BBC's education correspondent Ken Macdonald talking to some students and a teacher in a school in Falkirk, whose views on the performance of the panel were not enthusiastic.

Mr Morton gave yet another assurance which later turned out to be misleading. Towards the end of the programme he said that 'the quality-assurance systems that the SQA has are as in previous years'. This brought a phone call to the BBC claiming that it was simply not true. Ken Macdonald found out that some probationer teachers had been markers – that is, newly qualified teachers who are not yet fully registered. This was denied and described as 'scaremongering', and yet it was later admitted by the minister in parliament on 6 September. Mr Macdonald also discovered that some school inspectors had been markers. They are nominally independent of the whole process, and most of them have not taught in a school for many years. That provoked indignation among teachers. But the most serious quality failing of all was the complete absence of the normal procedure by which computer checks are run to ensure that the results on the certificates broadly correspond to the predictions that teachers had been making. In technical jargon these are referred to as 'concordances'. Ken Macdonald reported this on 31 August: 'Normally, how pupils actually perform in an exam is compared with how their school expects them to do. The computer compares that in turn with how accurate the school's predictions have been in the past. The checks can mean grades being improved – or failures converted to passes – before the results are issued. They can also highlight problems with marking. But this year, the SQA says, the checks were run on only a limited number of old-style Highers and Standard Grades because school predictions weren't available. And they weren't run at all for the new Highers. It could be a factor in the widespread reports of pupils whose grades are unexpectedly poor – and the anticipated large number of appeals.'

The magnitude of the discrepancies was confirmed by the stories which had been coming from schools. For example, a few days earlier, Tony Conroy, headteacher of St Ninian's High School in Kirkintilloch, had told *The Herald* that his school had been expecting 44 per cent of students to pass three or more Highers, whereas only 32 per cent did so.

That something like this had gone wrong was known to the Education Department and the SQA, although this fact was not released until much later, during the inquiry which the Scottish parliament launched into the events. On 9 August, as the results were going out, a senior statistician at the SQA emailed the Education Department to report that the pass rate for Highers was 65.3 per cent. This was some 5 per cent down on 1999. Indeed, you have to go back to the 1970s to find a pass rate as low as that. Alarms bells were ringing inside the SQA and the Department, and during August and September the SQA refused repeated requests by journalists to issue the pass rate (even thought it is normally issued at the same time as the results). A quick calculation would have provided the Department with a rough-and-ready estimate of the scale of the disaster. If there really was a 5 per cent underestimate of the proportion gaining a pass (which requires at least a C) then the chances are that there would be a similar level of error at each of the other grades in the Higher: A, B and D. So a 15 to 20 per cent error rate overall might not be so bad as an initial approximate guess at the extent of what had gone wrong. That figure would have been broadly consistent with the 80 per cent success rate that had been forecast by the SQA insider in June, and with the 16 per cent error rate reported by the universities' admissions service on 17 August.

These errors triggered an unprecedented number of appeals by students against the grades they had been awarded. The level of 'urgent' appeals was nearly 13 times the normal number of about 500 – that is, appeals from people who needed to get results for admission to higher education in autumn 2000. The level of other appeals at Higher Grade was nearly three times the normal number of just under 20,000. The processing of these took until late autumn, and dealing with appeals in the other parts of the exam system – Intermediate Grades and Standard Grades – took till Christmas. The markers required for this were teachers taken away from their normal classroom duties during the autumn. Although the government compensated schools financially for this loss, they could not guarantee that there would be no disruption to teaching, which there almost certainly was. It was estimated that about 800 to 900 markers were needed in total. Schools had to recruit temporary 'supply' teachers, of whom there are only about 1,400 in the whole of Scotland, to cover the markers' classes while they were away. Some schools must have had to employ supply teachers to cover subjects they were not qualified to teach: they would be, in effect, no more than child-minders. The long-term damage of that on students' progress will be impossible to estimate.

The appeals process forced the issue back underground again for a few weeks, but it resurfaced on the political front. Sam Galbraith made a statement to parliament on 6 September which mostly just repeated points that were already well known. Then the parliamentary inquiries got under way – from the Education committee and from the Lifelong Learning committee – which provoked a stream of written and oral submissions throughout September and October.

'A DISASTER'
The memorable aspect of the developing story in August 2000 was that the scale of the chaos was immediately apparent to teachers, very quickly evident to students and rapidly appreciated by journalists – and yet official assurances were repeatedly issued that matters were not really as bad as they seemed. But, in due course, the public statements caught up with the reality. Donald Dewar, prematurely back at work as First Minister after the heart

trouble that would kill him a month later, agreed that the whole episode had been 'a disaster' in an interview with the *Daily Record* on 11 September, one month after his education minister Sam Galbraith had told the same paper that 'it's a bit of a mess but I think we are getting over it', and had insisted to *The Scotsman* that 'it was important not to over-react and undermine public confidence'. The EIS, despite its initial caution, conceded on 28 August that the situation was 'a disaster'. And the same word was used by Mary Mulligan, convener of the Scottish parliament's Education committee on the radio programme *Good Morning Scotland* on 27 September, but at least she had been calling for an inquiry right from the beginning.

So a disaster it seems to be. The rest of this book looks deeper into the nature of the chaos and where it came from. Was the failure to issue correct results the only problem, or were there deeper questions with Higher Still? Has the response to the summer's events been adequate? And what lessons can we learn about the best way forward for Scottish education?

CHAPTER 2

The Highers: 'The Holy of Holies'

The Higher Grade examination is the cornerstone of Scottish secondary-school education. It is the culmination of a dozen years of schooling, the main summing up of a student's entire school career. It is also the main route by which students enter higher education, a veritable rite of passage. It is a cultural icon. It has been around for 112 years in some form or other, and so has become embedded in the national consciousness. The universal colloquial term for the exam – the Highers – has even achieved the status of an entry in the *Concise Scots Dictionary*.

No wonder, then, that it has been described as 'the Holy of Holies'. That was the phrase used by one of the most influential people in twentieth-century Scottish education, John Brunton, who was senior chief inspector of schools between 1955 and 1966, a time – like the present – of crucial transition. He used the expression in an interview he gave to Andrew McPherson and Charles Raab, for their book on how Scottish education is governed. Looking back on the 1950s, Brunton went on: 'Teachers, and indeed the public at large, understand this examination, and changes in it were a matter of public interest and understanding, and could meet with fairly ready acceptance. Consequent changes in the curriculum could also be accepted, provided they did not fundamentally alter the examination, regarded as the gateway to the universities and to success in the professions.'

Not much had changed by the year 2000: the immense public concern over the problems in issuing results showed that the social significance of the exam had, if anything, increased since Brunton spoke. It really was a crisis affecting the heart of Scottish education and Scottish culture.

This chapter looks at the history of the Highers. How did they acquire the significance which Brunton attributed to them and which hundreds of thousands of people still felt acutely in the summer of 2000? How could a mere examination generate such passionate debate about an entire system of education? What kind of education system – and what kind of culture – did the traditional Higher exam underpin, and how were these changing with the new kinds of Higher that were taken for the first time in that fateful year?

SCOTTISH EDUCATION AND SCOTTISH CULTURE

Education in Scotland is not just an important topic of social policy. It is not just a means of training people, not just the way in which young people are socialised into adult life. It is all these things, of course, but it is more than that. It is a core cultural symbol of the nation, and has been for at least a century and a half.

Historically there are three main reasons for this. The first is the capacity of education to give people opportunities in life – to foster the social mobility by which young people get access to better jobs than their parents had. Scots traditionally venerated education for this purpose above all. To get a flavour of that, consider this quotation from the report of the mid-nineteenth-century inquiry into Scottish education that was headed by the Duke of Argyll: 'The theory of our school system was to supply every member of the community with the means of obtaining for his children not only the elements of education, but such instruction as would fit him to pass to the burgh school, and thence to university, or directly to the university from the parish school.'

This was an overwhelmingly male world (girls did not even begin to get this kind of access to mobility until well into the twentieth century) and the opportunities were never open to more than a highly selected few – the so-called 'lads of pairts', the poor but academically able boys who could take the route which Argyll sketched. But, restricted though these routes were, they did exist, and, in the nineteenth century, probably more so than in most other countries in Europe. As a result, not only did Scotland have more university places per head of population than almost all other European countries, but the proportion of students from working-class or peasant backgrounds was, in the opinion of the historian R.D. Anderson, without parallel anywhere in the continent.

It was a highly competitive system, in which examination played a central role. The ethos was admiringly summed up in 1932 by Walter Elliot, later a Unionist Secretary of State for Scotland: 'It is a heritage wherein discipline is rigidly and ruthlessly enforced, but where criticism and attack are unflinching, continuous, and salt with a bitter and jealous humour. It is a heritage wherein intellect, speech and, above all, argument are the passports to the highest eminence in the land.'

It divided students into the select few and the damned majority, which brings us to the second historically important aspect of Scottish education: religion. The Protestant Reformation of 1560 in Scotland was, in the long run, a profoundly democratising influence, not least in the aspiration of its leader, John Knox, to establish a school in every parish, a high school in every town and a university in every city. An educated laity was needed for the presbyterian ideal of church government – so that every member of the congregation could understand the Bible and so that the men among them would be able to take part in the election of the minister. Knox's education system was more or less fully established in Lowland Scotland by the middle of the eighteenth century. It took rather longer in the Highlands, and was accompanied there by systematic official attempts to wipe out the Gaelic language.

The full rigours of Knox's vision had diminished somewhat by the middle of the nineteenth century, and the Argyll report found the parish schools also attempting to educate Catholic as well as Protestant children. By 1918 the original religious impulse had abated sufficiently for the separate schools that the Catholic Church had set up and maintained over several decades to be brought wholly within the public sector, where they remain to this day. But, although the character of the church influence on Scottish schools thus changed, the essentially religious character of the education system was barely touched by the 1950s. Schools instilled a sense of duty, both a moral duty to follow the precepts that the church – whether Protestant or Catholic – sanctioned, and a social duty to serve society. That social duty very definitely extended to the successful as well as the powerless. The students who did rise through the system to positions of wealth and power were encouraged to feel a sense of responsibility to those who had not had such luck – luck of intelligence, or luck in having the inclination to work hard.

So the education system of the late twentieth century was the immediate inheritor of a thoroughly religious tradition. The religion itself had declined, but the moral and social ideas still pervaded Scottish life. It is from that tradition that the Scottish predilection for public solutions to political problems ultimately comes – notably, the Scottish antipathy to the governments of Margaret Thatcher and John Major in the 1980s and 1990s, an antipathy which was the main background reason why people voted overwhelmingly to set up a parliament in the referendum of 1997. It is no wonder, then, that the education system is widely felt to be public property. What goes on inside a set of institutions that shape society in this way must be of enormous concern to the population in general, not just to the professionals and politicians who run it.

And that's the third historical significance of Scottish education, and perhaps the best known nowadays: politics. The autonomy of Scottish education was, in effect, guaranteed by the Treaty of Union of 1707, whereby the Scottish and English parliaments united into the new parliament of Great Britain. Education itself is not explicitly mentioned in the Treaty, but the Church is. Its independence was guaranteed by an associated Act of the Scottish parliament in the autumn of 1706, which was endorsed by the Treaty, and that Act gave the Church complete control over the appointment of teachers in the schools and professors in the universities. It also gave the Church the ultimate authority on the educational curriculum. So educational autonomy was a by-product of ecclesiastical independence.

Whatever the origins, however, there then gradually grew a sense that education was one of the three pillars of Scottish independence in the Union. Along with the Church and the law, education helped make Scotland unique, and kept at bay what was frequently felt to be the risk of anglicisation by our larger neighbour – not because England, on the whole, wanted to impose its will, but rather by neglect, by the familiar easy equating of Britain with England and vice versa. It was hardly surprising that education could be felt to be such a bulwark against that absorption. By it, nineteenth-century Scots could demonstrate their intellectual prowess to their partners in the Empire. They could attract some of the best English students to their distinguished ancient universities, and could send their own intellectuals south to help to shape Victorian culture itself.

In the twentieth century the political motivations changed but the cultural centrality remained. In the era of the centralised welfare state, it seemed to be all the more important to defend the distinctiveness of Scottish education in order to defend Scotland itself. As overt political power passed to the central state – through nationalisation, and the centralisation of pensions and the social-security system – the importance of maintaining the distinctiveness and autonomy of Scotland through cultural means seemed all the greater. Education spanned that divide between culture and politics. It came with the authority of the state, which funded and oversaw nearly all of it. In particular, the state continued to lend its weight to the exam system, as we will see later. But it was also cultural, and so was firmly Scottish. The main way it was cultural was not so much through the curriculum – which increasingly shared features with the curriculum in many European countries, including England – as by means of the culture of the teachers and the infrastructure. Nearly all the teachers were educated in Scottish universities or teacher-training colleges. One thing they continued to get there at least until the 1960s was a philosophical education, and – in the colleges – a prominent concern with the theory and practice of testing. Modern assessment methods were more or less invented in Scotland in the 1920s and 1930s, above all in the work of Godfrey Thomson, professor of education at Edinburgh University and principal of Moray House College in the city, and their legacy in the training courses lasted for many decades.

Scottish education has also been firmly Scottish in its governance, long before the Scottish parliament was created or even much thought of. This is discussed much more thoroughly in Chapter 5, which gives the political background to the exams crisis in 2000, but the main point for the moment is that the detailed rules by which the system operated were set in Scotland. Until the 1980s, educational legislation barely intruded into the classroom – a point that is difficult to imagine after the legislative zeal of the recent Conservative and Labour administrations. A senior inspector such as John Brunton was much more influential on the character of Scottish education than were the politicians who were ostensibly in charge. The key players politically were the inspectorate nationally, its advisors in various national quangos and committees, the directors of education in the local authorities (which actually run the schools), the national associations of headteachers, the trade unions representing teachers (especially the Educational Institute of Scotland, by far the largest) and the principals of the colleges and universities. These have been referred to by one writer, Professor Walter Humes, as the 'leadership class', an apt term for a tight policy-making community.

So the starting point for understanding the significance of the Highers is the more general significance of Scottish education in the nation's identity. Education has shaped Scottish culture, and been shaped by it, for a very long time, and has been felt to be what has made Scotland unique. Since the Highers stand at the apex of that system, education's importance makes them inescapable as a cultural icon too.

THE HIGHERS: EARLY YEARS

So exactly what are these supremely important examinations? And why were they invented?

The first Highers were sat in 1888. They came about because of highly disruptive change in the nature of schooling and universities in the preceding decades. The old parish-school tradition – the Reformation's legacy – was decaying, especially because of the massive growth of cities and large burghs during the Industrial

Revolution. Parish schools worked well in the essentially rural country of the pre-industrial period, but did not work in the mushrooming urban settlements of the nineteenth century. In the rural areas, all social classes continued to attend the local school – the persistence of the traditional Scottish system. But in the cities there was increasing pressure from the new middle class to found a network of secondary schools in which their sons (and soon also their daughters) would have the same kinds of educational opportunity as their rural counterparts, without having to attend the cheap and rather inadequate mixture of parish schools and other types of provision in the working-class districts.

This secondary-school movement gradually gained momentum so that by the 1880s there were some 60 full secondaries throughout the country (many fewer than the 450 or so today). But that then began to raise difficult questions for the Scottish universities. As our quotation from the Argyll commission earlier showed, they had traditionally taken students directly from the parish schools, frequently as young as 14. But the students coming from secondaries were 17 or 18, were more mature and had a more advanced education.

The universities themselves were under considerable pressure to modernise their curriculum and examinations in the face of competition from the new civic universities of London, northern England and Wales, as well as from the renovated Oxford and Cambridge. The key moment in this battle was the Northcote-Trevelyan report in 1853 which advocated a new style of recruitment to both the home and the imperial civil service: henceforth, it would be by competitive examination, not by nepotism and other forms of indefensible practice. By the end of the century, around three quarters of higher civil servants were graduates, over half, in fact, from Oxford or Cambridge. As Harold Perkin has put it in a history of the professions in Britain, the status of the professional middle class in general 'depended on persuading the public that they had a disinterested service to offer', and that seemed to be most effectively achieved by demonstrating through university studies that they had an aptitude for public office. The Scottish universities were profoundly influenced by this important source of employment for their graduates: they had to introduce their own entrance examination, a more specialised syllabus, and a stronger requirement that students actually graduate rather than merely attend individual classes as had been the norm.

These two changes – the expansion of secondary education, and the reform of the universities – were forced to pay attention to each other by the new Scotch Education Department, founded in the 1870s, and coming under the wing of the new Scottish Office after 1885. ('Scotch' was not changed to 'Scottish' until the Education Act of 1918.) It was an early instance of the Scottish leadership class asserting its authority. The key figure was Henry Craik, civil service head of the SED from 1885 to 1904, politically conservative (and in fact later a Scottish Unionist MP), but culturally a Scottish patriot. His vision was of a national Scottish leaving certificate that would, at one and the same time, be the aim of all the best students in the growing number of secondaries, and the main means by which the universities selected whom to admit. Such a standardised examination was needed as an aid to school inspection: it would give the inspectors, who were attached to the SED, a standard measure of the quality of individual schools.

Craik was an admirer of similar developments in France and especially Germany, whose new industrial and military prowess seemed to depend on a massive investment in state-sponsored education. Scottish Unionists such as Craik had few of the difficulties with using the state to promote national development that Conservatives in England had, because of the tradition of presbyterian belief in social responsibility. Craik himself was the son of a Glasgow minister, and had studied at both Glasgow and Oxford universities, and so he knew the most academically successful parts of both Scottish and English education very well.

Craik got his way. He proposed in 1886 that the examination should give 'considerable freedom of choice as to subjects', but that it should cover the main arts subjects offered in the Scottish universities. Its purpose would be to aid in the inspection of the secondaries: as he put it, the inspectors should root out 'any superficial knowledge which has not been based upon systematic training'. In the words of Henry Philip, who wrote the definitive history of the Highers in 1992, on which I have drawn heavily in this account, 'Craik saw the importance of stating aims and laying down standards if secondary education was to be established on a firm footing'.

Craik's proposals were not without their critics. The rector of Kelvinside Academy in Glasgow prophetically noted that 'if percentages become an all-powerful factor in school work, more harm than good will be done. Teachers will then be under strong temptation to give their energies to rote-work and cram.' The universities would have preferred to have operated their own system, through an examining board that they would have controlled. But Craik won, and the first exam, arithmetic, went ahead on Monday, 18 June 1888. Twenty-nine schools took part, ranging from Elgin in the north to Kirkcudbright in the south, taking in Dundee, Glasgow and Edinburgh on the way. There were 972 candidates.

Right from the start there was controversy over fairness. Philip cites *The Scotsman* claiming that the first maths exam was more difficult than had been recent papers for the MA degree at Edinburgh University. Nevertheless, the same newspaper also praised the SED for introducing an examination that could not 'be met by mere cramming, but only by careful and systematic training of the mental powers'. Craik himself was well pleased. His new exam would encourage the secondaries to concentrate their work on coherent goals. 'Scotch parents recognise the value' of secondary schools, he wrote, and would be willing to pay for them, through fees. The able but poor student would be admitted through endowments: 'The more it is recognised that these schools have a real educational value of their own, and are not merely a little higher on the social scale, the less will be the popular objections to such use of endowments.'

The popularity of the leaving certificate grew rapidly: within three years the number of schools using it had grown from 29 to 50, and the number of candidates from 972 to 3,120. This expansion then immediately raised the question of whether nonsecondary schools could take part. Philip quotes the EIS arguing in 1889 that restricting the certificate to students in secondary schools was unfair, especially since secondaries were available only in some geographical areas, and charged fees. The union praised the parish-school tradition, and said that the national system of elementary schools that had resulted from the 1872 Scottish Education Act was perfectly capable of administering the new exams as well. Craik and the SED responded by proposing what eventually became established – two decades later – as the norm: that elementary and secondary schools should be recognised as two distinct and sequential stages of education, not rival systems catering for potentially similar kinds of students. Through a series of quite complex changes, mostly overseen by Craik's equally powerful successor John Struthers, what eventually emerged by the early 1920s was a single certificate recording examination achievement at two levels – Highers and Lowers. Until 1950 these were awarded as a 'group certificate' – that is, students had to achieve passes (at one of these levels) in a prescribed range of subjects, and would be awarded nothing at all if they failed to do so. For example, in the regulations of 1912, to gain a certificate, students had to pass English, another language, and either maths or a science at Higher grade, and one further subject at either Higher or Lower grade. From 1902 until 1925 there was also an Intermediate Certificate, strongly advocated by those who favoured wide access to secondary education and the universities, but the SED eventually achieved its wish to abolish this in favour of tests of young people's aptitude at age 12. Only those who performed at a sufficient level would be allowed to enter secondary school, and those who did not would remain in the 'advanced divisions' of elementary school until they were permitted to leave at the age of 14, without any access to national certification.

SECONDARY EDUCATION FOR ALL
Given these controversies over the SED's initially successful attempts to restrict access to the secondary schools, and thereby to the leaving certificate, it was not surprising that the next phase

of debate was about extending some form of secondary education for all. That slogan had been coined by the socialist R.H. Tawney in England in 1922, and was also being advocated at the same time by William Boyd, head of the education department of Glasgow University. The basis for a much broader system was in fact laid by the 1918 Scottish Education Act. The sociologist and historian Andrew McPherson has noted its significance for the whole of the rest of the twentieth century in five respects. It allowed for the extension of compulsory education from 14 to 15: this established that there was no barrier, in principle, to the majority of children making a success of secondary education (although in practice the leaving age was not raised until 1947). Second, it asserted the principle of compulsory and publicly funded education and training for students aged 15 to 18 who had left school; this was not seriously attempted in practice until the late 1990s. Third, it made the local governance of education more efficient and powerful, by reducing the 987 local school boards to 38 education authorities, and giving them responsibility for all public sector schooling beyond the primary stage (as well as all the primary schools which the previous boards had governed). Fourth, the authorities were permitted to gain control of the Catholic schools, which, as we have already seen, they quickly did. And fifth, these education authorities were given the right to spend money to promote what we would now call equal opportunities.

The 1918 Act was therefore potentially revolutionary in its implications. Perhaps not surprisingly, then, the full implementation was resisted by the SED, under both Conservative and Labour governments. Its main argument was that pupils fell into two clearly defined groups: those who could benefit from a full secondary education (that is, as far as the leaving certificate) and those who could not. The latter group was estimated to be by far the larger – in Craik's view, for example, some 85 to 90 per cent of the population. The ideas thus promulgated took a long time to die, their residue lasting until the introduction of comprehensive secondary schooling in the 1960s, but they were resisted from the start. One reason, as the historian John Stocks notes, was simply demographic. To make a reality of this rigid separation between the academic and the non-academic would have required at least two post-primary schools in every community in Scotland, which would have been impossibly expensive in the straitened economic circumstances of the late 1920s. But the other was based on the same expansionist philosophy of the 1918 Act – as Stocks puts it, 'the [SED's] policy itself was out of tune with the wishes of parents and the views of the articulate section of the Scottish public'. Parents saw the 'practical' classes proposed by the SED as second-rate, and there was a broad view that rigid separation at age 12 would exacerbate social class divisions. 'At root,' writes Stocks, 'there was conflict over educability: the department's pessimism about the small number who were able to profit from secondary education was not generally shared.'

It was a sign that the meaning of secondary education had become widely accepted that this period was a time of stability in the leaving certificate. The debates were over access to it, not over its character. By 1939 the number of pupils taking part in the exams had grown substantially – reaching 7,898 (more than eight times the figure half a century earlier) – which was nevertheless still only about 5 per cent of the age group. The basic regulations remained much the same, although the grouping requirements for being awarded a certificate were adjusted. In this period there was also established the principle that the subject called English was at the core of secondary education. Until 1940 this was interpreted broadly, including not only language but also literature, history and (for a while) geography. Although history and geography were separated off then, literature remained, and it also remained common for teachers of English to possess a qualification to teach history as well. The intention of English was that students would gain not only the capacity to express themselves, especially in writing, but also a broad understanding of culture and moral philosophy. We cannot understand the controversies over English in the reformed exams of 2000 without noting this precedent: English has been interpreted in this humanistic fashion for at least 80 years.

POST-WAR EXPANSION

The 1945 Scottish Education Act consolidated the compromise over secondary education that had been evolving from the tensions between the Scottish Education Department and the principles of the 1918 Act. There would be a system of senior and junior secondary schools, the former taking students through to the leaving certificate at age 17, the latter stopping at age 15; allocation between these was decided at the age of 12, on the basis of the 'qualifying exam'. This remained divisive, but on the other hand did accept the principle of secondary education for all. There were serious attempts to articulate a distinct educational philosophy for junior secondaries, based on a coherently thought-out vocational education. The most notable example was during the reign of Brunton in the late 1950s, based on a 1955 report that recommended a broad education as the best basis for vocational training just as much as for academic study.

Despite these attempts, however, only senior secondary schooling – and the leaving certificate – were popularly regarded as real secondary education. The powers of the education authorities to spend money on promoting equal opportunities then encouraged a slow expansion of the senior secondaries, so that by the end of the 1950s some two fifths of the age group were in them. By that time, the grouping of the Higher certificate had been ended, which encouraged a greater proportion of the senior secondary population to attempt it: by the early 1960s, the proportion passing at least one Higher had risen to one in six, some three times the proportion gaining the group certificate in 1939 (although the proportion passing at least four Highers was still not much more than then, at 7 per cent).

This continuing selection became increasingly controversial, partly because it was still strongly related to the social class of pupils. For example, proportionately seven times as many middle-class pupils passed a Higher as working-class pupils. What is more, even among pupils who had performed quite well at the end of primary school, there was a sharp social-class divide in access to senior secondaries. One study in 1958 found that twice as many middle-class pupils of average ability entered senior secondaries as working-class pupils of the same ability.

A clear philosophy for ending this divided system had come as early as 1947, in a justly renowned report of the Advisory Council on Scottish Education. This was an official body, the sixth in a series that had been appointed since the early years of the century. The committee had been charged by Tom Johnston, the Labour Secretary of State for Scotland during the war, with considering what kind of secondary education was needed in an era of mass democracy (which, although dating from 1928, was still, because of the war, felt to be very new). It took up this challenge enthusiastically, restating eloquently the 1918 principle of broad access to secondary education as the necessary basis of democracy: 'It is clear that the marriage of freedom and order which democracy presupposes is possible only for a people conscious of its inheritance, united in purpose, and proof against the attacks of sophistry and propaganda; and that these qualities require not merely a literate, but an educated, nation.'

Two features of the report show how it was open to original thinking. The first was about the organisation of secondary education, where it proposed simply to end the distinction between senior and junior secondaries. It invoked what had always been the practice in small-town and rural Scotland: because it would have been too costly there to build separate secondaries, all pupils attended the same 'omnibus' school, although being quite rigidly grouped by academic ability into distinct 'streams'. The committee believed that this system could be made to work in urban areas too. It was a proposal for a system of comprehensive secondary education in all but name.

The other radical proposal was to do away with external examinations altogether – that is, exams set and marked by an agency outwith the individual school (the supreme example of which was, of course, the leaving certificate). It distinguished between external exams and the important and inevitable examination which the teacher carries out with his or her own pupils as part of their normal work. This, the report said, was as much an intrinsic part of any decent education system as the curriculum itself. It then raised three objections to external exams. First, they 'exalt the written above the spoken, magnify memory and mastery of fact at the expense of understanding and liveliness of mind'. Second, the examination 'depresses the status of the non-examinable', such as 'the aesthetic and creative side of education'. And, third, 'the examination which began as a means, becomes for many an end in itself'. Altogether, then: 'The examination has proved all too congenial to the hard practicality of the Scot, and in excessive concern about livelihood, the art of living has been forgotten.'

So pupils should be examined by their own teachers only. The report recommended that consistency across the country should be maintained by periodically checking up on teachers' marking standards by means of a uniform test taken by all pupils in every school, and then using that as the basis of an elaborate statistical procedure for adjusting the marks of teachers in the tests they set themselves. The key point would be that pupils were not judged by the uniform test: that was solely for the purpose of giving guidance to teachers on the standards expected. The pupils would be assessed by the examinations which their own teachers devised.

Here was a truly revolutionary challenge to some of the central traditions of Scottish education – that education should be about offering opportunities for successful professional careers to the most academically able, and that the mechanism for doing so should be an externally controlled and nationally standardised examination system. What is more, the committee was hardly dominated by dissidents or outsiders. The main author of the report, Sir James Robertson, was rector of Aberdeen Grammar School, and had sat on numerous other official committees set up by the SED. So the educational and political radicalism of the recommendations illustrates that even the dominant Scottish educational traditions are complex.

Nevertheless, neither proposal was immediately attractive to government or teachers, although the idea of a common system of secondary schooling did quite quickly become Labour policy after the party lost power in the 1951 general election. During the war years, teachers had been involved in actually administering the exams, but they were ready to return control to the SED in

1946. They were partly brought back in as markers from 1959 onwards, and in 1965 as members of advisory panels on the examinations in each subject. But the main developments until the early 1960s continued to be the expansion in access to the leaving certificate that had started in the late 1920s. One notable proposal for reform from the SED failed: the idea of a special advanced course to be taken by students who stayed at school for a year beyond their leaving certificate. This would have resembled the new A-level that was being introduced in England and Wales in the 1950s, but the proposal was shelved on the grounds that the standard it would have required would have been too high for all but a small minority of students.

THE O-GRADE AND THE EXAMINATION BOARD

Three major changes took place in the examination system in the 1960s. The first was the introduction of the Ordinary Grade, paralleling the English Ordinary Level which had been introduced in 1951. The absence of any similar qualification in Scotland had resulted in a high drop-out rate from courses that were supposed to lead to the leaving certificate, and this was increasingly seen as wasteful. So the O-grade was eventually introduced in 1962 as a means of consolidating the rationale for the divided system of secondary education: if wastage from the senior secondaries could be reduced, pressure to abolish them could be resisted. The new examination was proposed by a working party set up by Brunton, and was to take the place of the Lower Grade examination that was still running alongside the Highers. It would normally be taken in the fourth year of secondary school. The idea was that able pupils would bypass it, proceeding straight to Highers in fifth year. Henry Philip describes the report of this working party as 'one of the most influential in the development of Scottish education'. It was important not only for its recommendation, but also for the composition of the working party itself – a partnership of the SED and the teaching profession, whereas previous reforms to Scottish education had emerged either wholly from the inspectorate, or from one of the advisory councils.

The new exam was put in place swiftly, and was initially aimed only at what the working party described as the top 30 per cent of pupils. It should be a coherent end-point to schooling in its own right: that arose from the desire to end wastage. And it should be based on the same assessment principles as the Highers – an externally set and marked exam. There would be no compulsory subjects, but pupils would normally take a broad range. English retained the cultural role which it had at Higher: 'We considered the advisability of subdividing English into English language and English literature but agreed to recommend that English should continue to be a single subject as at present. The study of literature in schools should be essentially the reading of good texts and should not be divorced from the rest of the work in English.'

The problem for the SED was that the examination proved just too successful. In 1964 just over a quarter of fourth-year pupils passed at least one O-grade. By 1976 this had grown to 60 per cent, double the proportion that the exam was aimed at. In the 1960s it was used not only in the senior secondaries but also in some of the junior secondaries, and thus was contributing to a slow undermining of the entire edifice of divided secondary schooling. It was an early example of how examination systems in themselves can encourage broad access, but only by coming to dominate the educational stages concerned.

The second main change in the 1960s was in the governance of the examination system. The exams had continued to be administered by the schools inspectorate, reflecting their origins as a device for aiding inspection, but with the advent of the O-grade the burden was becoming immense. There was also a more democratic motive – a feeling that the social acceptance of the exams depended on their being administered by a fairly broad range of representative people. The idea of an independent examination board came from another working party set up by the SED, and so the recommendation could be presented as coming from independent advice. A broad composition of the governing body was written into the founding regulations in 1963. The board was charged with offering advice on examination policy as well as with actually running the exams, and so performed something of the function of the old advisory councils.

Nevertheless, it was a highly constrained democratisation. In the words of Andrew McPherson and Charles Raab, in their history of policy-making, 'The Secretary of State took powers of direction over the board, and created a powerful channel of influence through his assessors.' The assessors were normally inspectors, and so they kept a close involvement in overseeing the exams even while withdrawing from the mechanics of setting and marking. The deliberations of the committee in this regard were under strong direction from the senior chief inspector, Brunton. What is more, the replacement of the series of advisory councils with specialised boards or committees of this sort – another was soon to follow for the curriculum – narrowed the scope of the advice they could offer. Never again in the twentieth century was there to be the broad philosophical critique and recommendations of the council that had reported on secondary education in 1947.

The third change was less momentous in the short term: the establishing of a new course and examination in school sixth year. The SED had continued to lobby for such a move, and the same working party as had recommended the setting up of a board was also charged with considering this question. The committee was chaired by the principal of St Andrews University, an important link because any advanced work in sixth year would be bound to have implications for the level of the courses that were offered in the first year of higher education. The working party insisted that the high academic standard of the Highers themselves should not be compromised: 'It is precisely the exacting standard of the Higher grade pass that has given the Leaving Certificate its prestige and value in the eyes of the public,' and they noted that the Certificate was popularly called 'the Highers' even during the long period of time when it included exams at lower levels as well (such as the Lowers). However, the committee found the sixth year 'ragged and diffuse'; this was not to be the last time that distrust of what officials saw as students' incoherent choices would emerge. So they recommended an Advance Grade course that would place a lot more emphasis on students' working on their own than the Higher courses did.

The outcome that eventually emerged in 1968 was a compromise. Despite the assurances of the working group, teachers feared a threat to the Higher, and feared also that any Advanced Grade would rapidly come to resemble the English A-level. It would become the standard means of access to university, and would narrow the curriculum just at the time when English educationalists were trying to find ways of broadening theirs. The new courses and exams were called the Certificate of Sixth Year Studies, and were accompanied by an insistence that the Higher was to remain the main entrance exam for university. As Andrew McPherson and Charles Raab point out, this allowed the board to claim that it was promoting the liberal idea of study for its own sake. However, entrance to the new courses was restricted to students who had already passed a Higher in the same subject, and as a result the proportion of the age group attempting them never rose much above one in ten: as late as 1998, for example, it was 11 per cent. The inspectors' perception that the sixth year remained unsatisfactory proved to be one of the main motives for the fundamental reforms of both fifth and sixth year that emerged in the 1990s, as we will see in the next chapter.

COMPREHENSIVE EDUCATION AND STANDARD GRADE
However important these examination reforms were in the 1960s – the O-Grade, the Certificate of Sixth Year Studies and the new governing arrangements – they were not nearly as crucial as the ending of selection between different types of secondary school. The move to comprehensives had been happening slowly since the 1950s, at the instigation of local authorities. Some of the pioneering early experiments were in England, notably in Leicestershire and London, and in Scotland one of the leaders was the Catholic Church, encouraging the building of comprehensive Catholic schools in Glasgow. But the striking feature of the development of the comprehensive policy after it was put in place by the Labour government in 1965 was how rapidly and uniformly it was adopted throughout Scotland. There were few of

the controversies that accompanied the reform in England, and by the late 1970s the Scottish public sector was wholly comprehensive. Probably one reason for the quick acceptance was the legacy of 'omnibus' schools in the rural areas: reorganisation in Scotland was essentially an urban matter. Another reason was the sheer determination of the SED. In one sense, this was an entirely administrative reform. No legislation was needed: there is no Act of Parliament that dictates the overall structure of secondary schooling in Scotland. It was a policy devised and implemented by the inspectorate, working with the local authorities. In the words of McPherson and Raab, 'One is struck by the power of the Scottish centre, when supported by the local authority, to implement decisive and uniform organisational change.'

The Scottish comprehensive schools were judged by most independent evaluations to be successful. They were found to have raised attainment for all social-class groups, but to have raised it most for working-class pupils. This seemed to be a confirmation of the reformers' hopes. Further research then showed further beneficial effects. Most notably, it became clear that the position of Scottish Catholics had been transformed by the ending of selection. Before reform, just 5 per cent of Catholic schools had been senior secondaries, even though about 19 per cent of Scottish pupils were Catholic; so the ending of selection opened up new opportunities. Comprehensive schooling raised the academic attainment of Catholics substantially; by the end of the 1990s, younger Catholics consequently had chances in the labour market that were indistinguishable from young people who were not Catholics.

The other main research evidence on the effect of comprehensive schooling was on the curriculum. The most immediate consequence of the ending of selection was to raise the question of the kinds of courses which a common school should offer. This question was made all the more acute when the school-leaving age was raised to 16 in session 1972–73. The response was to set up yet more inquiries. The curriculum for ages 14–16 was considered by a committee chaired by James Munn, rector of Cathkin High School, and later chairman of the Curriculum Council that advised the government on curriculum matters in general. The other committee was on the examinations that would assess these courses, and was chaired by Joseph Dunning, principal of Napier College in Edinburgh.

The report of the Munn committee re-asserted the Scottish tradition of a broad curriculum, and proposed to take advantage of comprehensive schooling to make this a reality for a much wider segment of the population. It chose to give modern expression to that tradition by means of the views of one of the most internationally influential thinkers on the curriculum in the last four decades, Professor Paul Hirst of London University. He believed that knowledge is organised into about eight 'modes', and the Munn report proposed that each student should experience all of these: language and literature, mathematics, science, social studies, creative and aesthetic studies, physical activity, religious studies and moral studies. The notion of domains of knowledge was also quite in keeping with the Scottish tradition: for example, until the 1960s, students in the first two years of the four older Scottish universities had to select their subjects from lists that broadly corresponded to the first four of these modes. In the universities there was, in effect, an additional philosophical mode as well, but, as we have seen, that role was played in the schools by English literature.

The Dunning recommendations were for a new certificate at age 16, replacing the O-grades, that would offer some form of appropriate assessment for all pupils. They also proposed important changes in assessment techniques, which we will return to in a moment. Both committees reported in 1977, and the ideas were accepted in principle by the early 1980s. The outcome was the Standard Grade exams and courses, which were introduced subject by subject, and were fully in place by the early 1990s. Scotland had then acquired a common curriculum at ages 14–16 that had aroused none of the controversies over similar reforms in England. By the early 1990s the results were exactly as the reformers had hoped: sharp reductions in gender and social-class differences in access to a broad curriculum.

These changes that accompanied comprehensive schooling

help to explain why it became and remained much more popular in Scotland than in the rest of Britain. By the 1990s only around a quarter of people in Scotland favoured a return to selection, in contrast to around a half in all regions of England. Surveys showed that people in Scotland (and parents) respected teachers and believed that they taught the basics well; there was thus no popular grounds for any political questioning of the comprehensive settlement. All the political parties represented in the Scottish parliament – including the Conservatives – broadly favour the principle of comprehensive schooling. Scottish educational history, the relatively smooth introduction of the reform, and the evidence that it had been successful all helped to establish a new consensus, always fairly easy in a small country with interlocking networks of policy-making and debate.

VOCATIONAL EDUCATION AND A FUNDAMENTAL CHANGE IN ASSESSMENT PHILOSOPHY

The last important reform of courses and assessment before the debate about the Highers in the 1990s was the introduction of new vocational awards from 1984 onwards. This was not an area in which Scotland had been particularly innovative until then, but the new context was the pressure from Margaret Thatcher's government to make schooling more relevant to the world of work. The flagship policy in this regard was the Technical and Vocational Education Initiative. This was a well-funded scheme, and so was potentially attractive to schools. But it was administered from Sheffield, and so threatened the autonomy of Scottish educational policy-making, and many teachers feared that it would undermine comprehensive education by creating separate vocational tracks.

The reaction to the TVEI showed the Scottish inspectorate at its most politically adept. It managed to secure a delay by a year in the implementation of the TVEI in Scotland, during which time it devised an entire new qualification, and a new body to oversee it: a suite of National Certificate modules, administered by a new Scottish Vocational Education Council. The inspectors insisted that in schools, TVEI fitted in with the developing Standard

Grade courses; in colleges TVEI had to be consistent with the National Certificate modules, and indeed schools themselves started to use them in fifth and sixth year, and even to a limited extent in third and fourth year.

The main immediate feature of the National Certificate was this political one. But two educational features had lasting significance. The first was its modular character. Instead of courses lasting a year or longer, learning was divided into 40-hour chunks. That may have seemed sensible in the vocational context in which it arose, but was to become highly contentious when proposals were made in the 1990s to apply the same organisational principle to all courses. The modular breakdown of courses has become one of the main controversies in the whole debate about reforming the Highers.

The other crucial principle in the National Certificate had even more profound implications, and was controversial even in the vocational training context for which it was devised. This was a change in assessment philosophy itself. Most of the examinations we have been surveying in this chapter have been based on two ideas: so-called 'norm-referencing', and the idea of an exam as a sampling of a culturally defined body of knowledge.

Norm-referencing means that students are judged by how they perform in comparison with the other people sitting the exam, rather than on the grounds of their own capacities. The alternative is usually called criterion-referencing, and the classic instance is learning to drive a car. In principle, everyone could pass their driving test, and whether an individual candidate is successful does not depend on how other candidates perform. In a norm-referenced test with a fixed pass rate, by contrast, an individual's chance of success depends on the quality of the other candidates in the same diet of exams.

Standard Grade assessment has tried to move some distance away from norm-referencing, but the National Certificates went the whole way, replacing it completely by the idea of 'competence'. Just as you are judged capable of driving a car if you demonstrate the necessary competence, so – in the field of vocational education – you are judged capable of being an electrician or a computer programmer if you prove that you are appropriately competent. It was felt that what was castigated as abstract learning in the classroom was at best vaguely relevant to real work settings. It was pointed out that this principle had always been applied in the high-status professions: lawyers, doctors, actuaries, teachers themselves and many others have always followed a course of practical assessment during placements in real workplaces, as well as the academic assessment of their performance in traditional exams.

This was not without controversy even in the vocational context, because the narrowly defined notion of specific competences led to the discarding of the old concept of skill, along with all the dignity that accompanied that. As John Fairley, a leading Scottish writer on vocational training, has pointed out: 'Skill, in the sense of the craft skills valued by the labour movement, was an objective characteristic of the worker. Competence, by contrast, was concerned with performance in relation to tasks.' What is more, whereas skill was acquired during a long period over the character of which workers themselves had influence, through their trades unions, 'competence and the means of acquiring it were likely to be defined by employers, or by "experts" brought in from the college or the personnel department'.

As we will see when we look at the debates about assessment in the reform of the Highers, this idea proved highly controversial when it was applied to non-vocational courses. And that was because of the second change to assessment philosophy which the idea of competence entailed. The traditional exams were based on the notion that part of the function of education is to distil the culture of a society, to pass it on to the next generation of students, and to assess their understanding by a sampling of that culture. So, for example, in the study of literature, although competences are important, they are a means to an end. Thus it is indeed highly important that students should be competent in the techniques of literary criticism – say, be able to dissect the metaphors used by Shakespeare in *King Lear*. That is something that could indeed be appropriately assessed by a philosophy of competence, just as would be a mathematician's ability to manipulate calculus, or a geographer's skill in map-reading, or a linguist's technical grasp of French grammar. But these competences, the critics argue, do not come anywhere near encapsulating the cultural and intellectual purpose of studying literature, mathematics, geography or French. Knowing that *King Lear* is full of animal imagery is no more than a means to the end of culturally understanding what the play has to say about the boundaries of human society. Calculus is no more than an intricate crossword puzzle unless it relates either to the uses to which scientists and engineers put it, or to the essentially philosophical and aesthetic ideas which underlie pure mathematics. Reading a map is pretty trivial (however difficult and necessary) compared to understanding the cultures of the places it designates. And conjugating French verbs is a poor substitute for understanding French culture.

These controversies were kept at bay during the 1980s, since the competency idea remained mostly confined to the training world. At first, the National Certificate did not seem to have any bearing on the Highers. But, as we will see, as more and more students in fifth and sixth year began to take modules, that assumption proved increasingly inaccurate. The controversies then exploded spectacularly in the development of Higher Still.

CONCLUSIONS

Five broad conclusions can be drawn from this survey of the intimately intertwined histories of Scottish education and Scottish examinations. The first is to reiterate the points made in the Brunton quotation which we saw at the beginning. Amidst all the many changes to assessment above and below the level of the Higher, the Holy of Holies remained largely untouched. The longer that went on, the more difficult it was to do anything about it. By the 1980s it had come to symbolise the continuity of Scottish education, and that in turn made it highly politically charged. When Margaret Thatcher was being accused of seeking to anglicise Scotland, the one thing that had to be held on to at all costs was the Higher, a totem in almost the literal sense of the term as an outward symbol of what made Scottish education distinct, and therefore of what made Scotland Scottish.

The second conclusion is that, despite the beginnings of change in assessment philosophy at Standard Grade, and the much more radical changes in the National Certificate, the philosophy on which the Highers were founded remained essentially unchanged. They had always been based on norm-referenced exams, sampling students' knowledge of an entire segment of culture. They are one of the oldest systems of nationally standardised public examination in Europe – roughly contemporaneous with the emergence of the French Baccalauréat and the German Abitur, but having gone through many fewer changes in the meantime, and some 60 years older than the English A-level. Their very dominance has shaped the school system. They have enforced what their supporters would see as a fixed point of high academic standards. They have also made Scottish education into what their critics prefer to see as a destructive, over-assessed competition.

Despite the critics, however, the story of the Highers during their first century was also inescapably linked to debates about access – the third conclusion. That started as soon as the exam was invented, when there was immediate pressure to extend some version or level of it to elementary schools as well as the new secondaries. The resulting expansion of secondary schooling was given important ideological support by the 1918 Act, which resulted in the slow acceptance of the principle of secondary education for all. Selection between types of secondary was the next barrier to wide access to the Highers, as was the O-grade. But comprehensive schooling and the sheer popularity of the O-grade then broke these barriers down. That encouragement was reinforced by Standard Grade and the National Certificate: as we will see in detail in the next chapter, by the early 1990s these had become the stepping stones by which a majority could, in principle, see Highers as potentially within their grasp. The apparently rather odd conclusion, then, is that assessment, even though widely criticised for being invidious and excluding, has actually been a force for democratisation. The very challenge of gaining passes, and the further opportunities which these confer in higher education or the labour market, have encouraged wider and wider groups of young people to raise their sights. It seems to be the inspiration of success that dominates, not the fear of failure.

That is why, fourth, the educational and political success of Scottish comprehensive secondary schooling probably depends on its academic character, in spite of the fears of its critics and the doubts of its supporters. Critics have alleged that comprehensives have dulled standards. The most enthusiastic supporters have claimed for 40 years or more that a truly comprehensive system, based on the needs of the individual learner, ought not to be so dominated by assessment as it has always been. But it may be precisely because Scottish comprehensives have been so focused on widening access to the Highers for the largest possible number of students that they have been popular and relatively successful academically. Take one very specific and measurable example: the historical disadvantage of girls in Scottish education. There has in fact been a long-standing willingness in Scottish educational culture to accord intellectually able girls an almost equal access to education. Their historical difficulty has been in getting their abilities recognised. So a nationally standardised and universally available examination system could be used as an opportunity by girls, with the results we now see – girls doing better than boys in almost all subjects, and gaining entry to university in at least equal numbers. The Highers have been, in that sense, an agent of emancipation – not the cause of it (which lies deep in the trans-formation of gender roles), but an important means by which it came about.

The credit, or blame, for all this has to be taken not just by the schools but also by the government department which planned every single step – the fifth and last conclusion. The Scottish Education Department has kept a tight control of the Highers since their inception, and the means by which it has done so is the schools inspectorate. No significant change in certification in the last 112 years has happened without the close involvement of the inspectorate, and it has actually instigated almost all of them. It has done so with very little recourse to the politicians, and with almost no use of legislation: assessment in Scotland is nearly all governed by technical rules and administrative arrangements, not by the law. This is real policy-making, real creativity in which the inspectorate is the undisputed leader. If Scottish education, and the Highers in particular, have any qualities worth admiring, then the inspectors must take a leading share of the credit. And if things go wrong, they cannot avoid some of the blame. But the striking feature of the first century of inspectorate supervision of the Highers was how tightly it did manage them. Very little went wrong, which is why, in the last analysis, the crisis of the year 2000 turned out to be so utterly disconcerting.

CHAPTER 3

Why Reform?

If one single explanation had to be given for why there was pressure to reform the Highers in the 1990s, it would be comprehensive secondary schooling. As we saw in the last chapter, this led to a rapid expansion in demand for meaningful courses and assessment at ages 14–16, and the partial satisfaction of that then simply fed the same demands into fifth and sixth year. In that sense, at least considering a reform of the Highers was not a mere whim of a government minister or a senior inspector of schools: it was a demographic inevitability.

But the character of the reform was not dictated by what had gone before, either in the sense of what shape would be taken by any new structure of courses and assessment, or in the content that these courses would have. To pick up again an example we used at the end of the previous chapter: student demand for post-16 courses and assessment would not, in itself, tell us whether *King Lear* would be a sensible subject of study in the English literature curriculum, and would not in itself determine how students' understanding of the play could be judged. Much of the debate about the reform of the Highers confuses these points. It is politically expedient in Scotland to say that the popularity of comprehensive schooling forced a reform of the Highers, but sliding from that into seeking to justify one particular version of reform is not valid at all.

This chapter, then, explains why pressure built up for a reform, outlines how the inspectorate and the Conservative government responded to the pressure, summarises the conclusion of the committee chaired by Professor John Howie which looked into the options for reform, and explains how his report was received when it was published just before the general election in 1992. If there is one overriding message from this chapter, it is that there were choices all along the way. Nothing that happened in the summer of 2000 was the inescapable outcome of these debates in the late 1980s and early 1990s. Conversely, the crisis that now faces the exam system does not, in itself, show that these debates were a waste of time, and certainly does not allow us to discard as worthless everything that was said at that time.

ORIGINS OF THE HOWIE COMMITTEE

The most thorough analysis of why a committee of inquiry into the Highers was set up, of what evidence it received, and of what conclusions it reached has come from Andrew McPherson, then a professor of sociology at Edinburgh University. It is worth dwelling for a moment on McPherson's significance in all this. As it turned out, he was one of the most eloquent critics of the Howie report that emerged. He had also been one of the main voices in the debate that was urging caution on the question as to whether a fundamental reform of the Highers was needed. He was in a position to make these points because of the influential work which he and his colleagues had carried out since 1972 at the Centre for Educational Sociology in the university. (I was one of his colleagues for a few years in the early 1990s.) Through a series of surveys of Scottish school-leavers, the CES had established itself as a world leader in the sociological study of young people's educational experiences, and former research associates of the centre had gone to occupy leading positions in governmental and international agencies, and in numerous educational faculties across Europe and North America.

McPherson, who has now retired, is a historian by origin, and so brought to his understanding of sociological issues a sense of the long perspective. That is why his works on educational policy-making, or on the comprehensive schooling issue, or on the significance of the Scottish university tradition, or more generally on education's impact on Scottish culture, remain so significant. (Some of his most important works in the present context are listed in the guide to further reading at the end of this book.) His voice in the debate about the Highers was not just that of another academic; it came from the most eminent sociologist of education that Scotland has produced.

Writing in the *Scottish Government Yearbook* in 1992, he identified two broad sources of the pressure for a committee of inquiry, each with several aspects. The first was the long-standing desire of the Scottish Education Department to do something about what the inspectorate considered to be the messy character of fifth and especially sixth year in secondary schools. We have already seen some of this in the previous chapter – the idea of an advanced course that was mooted in the late 1940s, the firmer proposals for an Advanced Grade in the early 1960s, and the compromise outcome in the Certificate of Sixth Year Studies in 1968. The problem had always been that if any new course took two years, replacing the Highers in fifth year, it would threaten the viability of small schools. That would have two awkward political implications. One would be in rural areas, where the average size of secondaries had always been well below what would be considered viable in England. As we have seen, the omnibus rural high school had come to be seen as the very embodiment of the Scottish tradition. The other problem was in the cities. Secondary schools serving districts of acute social deprivation tended to be small, and became even smaller after the Conservatives in 1981 had given parents much greater freedom to decide which school their children would attend.

The vocational National Certificate which was introduced after 1984 did help to postpone dealing with the problem. Comprehensives had encouraged much higher proportions of young people to stay on beyond age 16 (up from 39 per cent in 1981 to 57 per cent in 1990), and the National Certificate was filling some of the curricular gaps for which the academic Highers were ill-suited. But the accusation continued to be made that this was a short-term expedient, not a coherent solution: as we have seen, the National Certificate was originally intended to be mainly about vocational education, and the expansion of it into areas traditionally reserved to the school curriculum – such as languages and even philosophy – was regarded as unsatisfactory by those who distrusted the competence-based assessment techniques on which the modules were based and what they saw as the Vocational Education Council's lack of expertise in devising curricula.

The second source of pressure came from the universities. The Highers started life partly as a university entrance exam, and had never lost that role. The drastic cut in university funding which the Conservative government had imposed in 1981 had begun to reduce their leading influence over post-16 schooling in general. Their four-year honours degree was under threat as more wasteful than the three-year courses available elsewhere in the UK. And they were facing stiff competition from the colleges of higher education that were centrally funded by the SED – places such as Napier College in Edinburgh, Paisley College and Robert Gordon's in Aberdeen. The universities chose to respond to these various pressures by restricting access: instead of allowing staff-student ratios to worsen, they made it more difficult for students to get in. The result, in McPherson's words, was that 'pupils whose fifth-year Highers would have been good enough to secure them entry to higher education from fifth year in the 1970s were obliged in the 1980s to return for a sixth year to upgrade their qualifications'. In consequence, the sixth year became increasingly like a remedial year, not at all the opportunity for using the CSYS as an induction into mature, independent study.

Despite all this, it was not until 1990 that the inspectorate took the decision to establish a committee of inquiry. That was partly for political reasons, and took place during one of the brief inter-ludes when Michael Forsyth did not have some sort of ministerial role in the Scottish Office. Mr Forsyth had not been persuaded of the need for reform, and was also acutely aware of the political dangers that tinkering with the Highers posed for an embattled Conservative government, especially after the party had lost half its Scottish seats and dropped to less than a quarter of the popular vote in the 1987 general election. Mr Forsyth was also suspicious of the power which interest groups such as the inspectorate wielded in Scottish public policy. But then, for a brief period, Thatcher made him Conservative Party chairman in Scotland, and his successor as education minister, Ian Lang, turned out to be much more in the traditional ministerial mode, and acceded to the inspectorate's wishes.

John Howie, the chairman of the committee, was professor of

mathematics at St Andrews University, and had come to the notice
of the inspectorate as a member of the Dunning committee that
had led to the Standard Grade. He was not a member of the
educational establishment and was not politically controversial.
His whole personal style, moreover, was likely to encourage
consensus – the very antithesis of the confrontations over Scottish
educational policy that the government was encountering elsewhere at the time (such as over the issue of compulsory national
testing of children in primary schools). The composition of
Professor Howie's committee also seemed to be aimed at securing
consensus. Contrary to the thrust of government practice in the
preceding decade, it contained no industrialists, and the closest it
got to the government's ideological preferences was a
representative of the Scottish Consumer Council. In fact, the
members were overwhelmingly from the educational world: it
could have been a committee of Scottish education at any time in
the previous half-century. It also was advised by the inevitable
inspectorial assessors, one of whom was the second most senior
inspector, Donald Mack.

The committee was given a fairly narrow remit: 'To review the
aims and purposes of courses and of assessment and certification
in the fifth and sixth years of secondary-school education in Scotland; to consider what structure of courses and what forms of
assessment best satisfy these aims and purposes, taking account of
the needs of pupils of varying ability and background, the
demands of employment and the requirements of, and developments in, higher and further education; and to recommend
necessary changes.' But as it worked its way through the evidence
it received, it gradually interpreted these tasks in a very broad
way indeed.

EVIDENCE SUBMITTED TO THE HOWIE COMMITTEE

The people who submitted evidence were overwhelmingly of the
view that change was needed. The first problem that was identified was that the Higher was not living up to its main role of
preparing students for entry to higher education. It was claimed
that students had to cram their learning into no more than two

terms of school (from August to April). It was claimed that schools then had no option but to teach superficially, developing in their students such poor techniques of studying that they were unable to take proper advantage of university courses when they entered them. Some school students, despite this cramming, would face what was further claimed to be the demoralising experience of failing a Higher in fifth year, and so would spend a large proportion of their time in sixth year retaking courses they had already followed.

The background reason for this was that the Higher was now being attempted by students who had a much broader range of abilities than the traditionally very academic students for whom it had always been intended. By 1990, in fact, 39 per cent of the age group were passing at least one Higher, which is at least four times the proportion that Henry Craik believed in the 1920s could benefit from these courses. In other words, the Highers were suffering the same fate that the O-grade exam had experienced in the 1970s, and, just as it had to be reformed, so allegedly did they.

The temporary expedient of offering fifth-year students National Certificate modules was also judged to be unacceptable because of the differing philosophies of assessment that we noted in the previous chapter. This, it was alleged, was thoroughly confusing, not just for the students, but also for staff in higher education institutions who were trying to select applicants to courses.

The main conclusion to which this evidence seemed to point was the abandonment of the one-year Higher altogether, amalgamating the Highers and the Certificate of Sixth Year Studies into a suite of two-year courses. Much of the public debate while Howie was taking evidence concerned this proposal. Such an idea would, it was claimed, get rid of the problem of the two-term dash to Higher. It would open up an opportunity for a more coherent curriculum, extending to the Highers the principles of independent study that were embodied in the CSYS. A two-year course would have the benefit of reducing the amount of examination pressure which students faced.

However, as Professor Howie himself frequently acknowledged

during the consultation period, that reform in itself could not deal with all the issues, because a two-year course would presumably be even less attractive to the growing population of students who stayed on beyond age 16 but who were not likely to be interested in attending university. As McPherson pointed out, one option would be to make the Highers course easier: if the option of resitting in sixth year were to be ended, that reduction in difficulty might be the only way to avoid a drop in the proportion qualifying for higher education. But deliberately reducing the difficulty of examinations was not politically acceptable in the climate of the early 1990s (and would be even less so today, as education ministers and inspectors strive ever harder to show how rigorous they intend to be). The other option would be to make the Higher available at several levels, as had happened with Standard Grade; as it turned out, and as we will see in the next chapter, this is in effect what happened with Higher Still. The third option would be to create two separate tracks as was common in other European countries – one predominantly academic, the other mainly vocational.

McPherson and colleagues (including myself) at the Centre for Educational Sociology argued against the two-year option, on two main grounds. The first was that what the inspectorate saw as the messiness of fifth and sixth year, far from being a problem, was actually a real strength of the Scottish system. It promoted choice. Lack of imposed coherence might be a disadvantage at earlier stages of schooling. But for young adults, and especially in an era when educational choice had become a by-word for politicians, the only coherence that should matter ought to be that which students themselves choose. Likewise, far from there being problems arising from the different assessment philosophy between the Highers and the National Certificate modules, this variety also enhanced choice. Students were finding their own way through the choices and judgements entailed in being able to assemble flexible groupings of modules, Highers taken in fifth year, Highers resat in sixth year, Highers sat for the first time in sixth year, and passes in the Certificate of Sixth Year Studies. There was no hard evidence of confusion at all. Indeed, insofar as increasing proportions of young people were voluntarily staying on into both fifth and sixth year, the evidence seemed to be that they relished what was on offer. That many would have been staying on because they needed further qualifications to get a job, or to get access to a post-school course, did not invalidate this point, but merely showed further that students could use the flexibility instrumentally, as a means of attaining their own desired goals.

The other argument against a two-year Higher was that the flexible fifth and sixth years promoted high post-compulsory participation. Evidence can be cited from many countries that students are encouraged to stay in education by the prospect of success, and by the knowledge that there are ways of compensating for partial failure. That is exactly what the old style of Scottish fifth and sixth year did. At the end of fourth year, a student of moderate academic ability would know that there was a variety of options if he or she stayed on in school – various possible combinations of Highers and modules. Because Highers were sat in fifth year, the sixth year was always available to recover from any disappointments in these first results. The fifth-year exams were what McPherson called a 'reality test' – allowing students to check on their progress, and to adjust their sixth-year programme to maximise the likelihood of their getting into whatever course they hoped to enter after school. The fifth-year exam also meant that students who stayed on were not committed to two years of education, which might be particularly important for families with little money to spare. Indeed, until the gradual replacement of student grants with loans in the 1990s, the option of entering university from fifth year was also important for this reason, because, once there, such students would receive public financial support. None of these advantages were available in a two-year system, such as with the A-level in England.

Since most of these arguments against a two-year system would have applied equally to separate tracks, the other option on the table, the CES case was in effect for an incremental adjustment to the status quo. In fact, the scope for slow adjustment to the existing structure of courses and assessment was part of that case. It was argued that the Highers should not be condemned on the basis of an isolated snapshot from one year. For example, in public meetings, Professor Howie frequently cited what he called the 'sad statistics' of failure among students in fifth year – for instance, the facts that, in 1990, one third of fifth-year students gained no Higher passes at all, and that a further 18 per cent gained only one. On the face of it, this seemed to indicate a system that was not serving students well. But, looked at over time, the statistics of Highers passes could be read differently, as a process of slowly extending opportunity to ever larger segments of the school population. Consider, for example, the proportion of students passing at least one Higher by the time they had left school. Taking into account results in both fifth and sixth year, this had doubled from just 18 per cent in 1965 to 38 per cent in 1989, and indeed in the late 1980s was rising by about 2 per cent per year. This steady increase, it was claimed by Howie's critics, showed that the old system was still working. Another way of putting that is to ask what the people who were getting just one Higher in 1989 – the 'sad statistics' – would have been getting two decades earlier. The answer for 1965 is that they would have been unlikely to have passed even one O-grade (only 30 per cent did so). So people who in the 1960s were below the threshold of gaining any certification at all were by the late 1980s gaining something, even though they were not among the academic stars.

The validity of this claim that the unreformed system had potential for further expansion can be retrospectively tested by asking whether it did in fact expand over the ensuing decade to the moment when the new Higher exams were introduced. The evidence is clear: it did. Rates of staying on beyond age 16 reached three quarters in the late 1990s, up from just over half in the late 1980s and from just over a third in the late 1970s. The proportion of school-leavers with at least one Higher Grade pass rose to 44 per cent in 1998. The proportion with three or more passes – informally the threshold for entry to university – had reached 30 per cent, up from 23 per cent in 1989, from 20 per cent in 1980, and from 12 per cent in 1965. In fact, in 1998 a higher proportion of the age group was reaching this university-entrance level than had been scraping just one O-grade in 1965. At the same time, research commissioned by the Scottish Office had shown that the standards of the Highers had remained broadly intact.

HOWIE'S RECOMMENDATIONS

When Howie's committee reported, in March 1992, it nevertheless found a consensus in favour of change. It found a wide agreement that certain principles had to be respected in any new examination system. The basis was curricular breadth: 'The committee wholeheartedly endorses Scotland's broad educational traditions and wishes to reaffirm them as the foundation for the future.'

From this it was inferred that students should have knowledge and understanding of themselves, of the physical world and of how societies operate. Students should have cognitive skills – notably linguistic skills, mathematical skills and thinking skills – and should know how to apply these. They should have 'social, interpersonal and personal skills', and should have the physical skills that are involved in sport, the arts and applied technology. They should be able to understand, evaluate and form views about moral dilemmas, including their social aspects (broadly what have later come to be described as 'citizenship skills'). They should be prepared for work and for life in democratic society. And education should pass on the cultural heritage: 'Students should be initiated into the main cultural achievements of their communities, both for their personal growth and for their role as potential contributors to the development of that culture.'

More specifically, Howie found agreement around the characteristics of a system in fifth and sixth year of school that would further these aims. It should be broad and deep. It should form links both with pre-16 education and with education and training beyond school. It should bridge the divide between academic and vocational study. It should encourage access to education, staying on beyond 16 and 18, and return to education by those who left prematurely. It should be efficient. And it should take account of the European dimension. This last was widely interpreted as code for: avoid the A-levels and look at models from elsewhere.

The consensus was overwhelmingly of the view that the existing system was inadequate and did not measure up to these standards. The report summarised five main deficiencies. First, it reiterated the points mentioned above about the full potential of the Highers not being available to more than a minority of students. Most students, it claimed, did not have coherent breadth in the courses they followed, and 'the Scottish system offered few opportunities for searching scholarship' – in other words, lacked the deep preparation for university study that the inspectorate had been striving for at several points during the previous 40 years. This problem was the consequence of the much more diverse character of the students who were now entering fifth year. Because comprehensive education had encouraged so much new staying-on beyond age 16, the old academic style of the Highers was no longer enough.

The partial response to this diversity that was represented by the National Certificate modules was no better than an ad hoc compromise. This led to the second deficiency. Most students had extensive experience of failure in fifth and sixth year, precisely because of the flexibility that the admirers of the current arrangements lauded. There was a lack of a 'steady gradient' from third year to sixth year: the gulf between Standard Grade and Higher was just too wide for many students. Far from the sixth year being a sign of well-planned flexibility, it was no better than an emergency fall-back for students who otherwise would have almost nothing to show for their school years. The shortness of the courses encouraged poor study habits.

Third, the flexible combination of Highers and modules had not really done anything to raise the status of vocational education, which remained a pariah alongside the traditionally very academic style of Scottish schooling.

Fourth, although the flexibility was undeniable, it was also wasteful. It prevented coherent planning of courses, it lowered expectations, and was inefficient in the sense that 'substantial numbers of students drop out in arbitrary ways in a fashion which limits the continuity and cohesiveness of teaching'.

Fifth, although the Scottish system might have stood up well compared to that in the rest of the UK, it looked weak in comparison with other European countries. The report claimed that 'the key feature of most continental systems is that students cover a broad, quasi-mandatory programme, so ensuring substantial coverage of a whole range of subjects or curricular areas'. Such programmes also often allow for the deep study of a few areas.

Not surprisingly, given this analysis and the consensus which lay behind it, the report then concluded that 'our system is seriously wanting in several respects', and so that 'the status quo is not an option'.

In a sense, that bit was easy, although the work of the committee in gathering together a consensus should not be underestimated. It really was a remarkably open style of consultation, quite untypical of the various committees on Scottish education which had sat over the years, and anticipating by a decade the deliberately open style that the Scottish parliament was later to encourage, such as in the 1999 inquiry into student finance chaired by Andrew Cubie. In that sense, Howie was a pioneer.

Much more difficult was making recommendations, especially given the further finding from the consultation that most Scottish opinion was against radical change. The committee decided to be very radical indeed, and very European. It recommended that there should be two 'pathways' starting in fourth year, a year earlier than the existing courses. In consequence, Standard Grade would be taken in third year, and the pace of learning in the first three years would be much more rapid. This was favoured by the committee because they had heard evidence from the inspectorate (although from almost no one else) that pupils marked time in first and second year at high school.

One of the pathways would be called the Scottish Certificate (abbreviated to Scotcert, in the barbarous style then in vogue, a style that would certainly have been unacceptable to all the previous reformers of Scottish education). It would come in ten forms, and would combine general and vocational elements. The ten would correspond to particular types of employment – for example, agriculture, construction, catering, caring, business and administration, and leisure and recreation. There would also be two 'general' versions, one arts-based and the other science-based. The components of all the versions would be intended to fulfil the general aims that the report had endorsed, such as acquiring the 'core skills': communication, numeracy, personal and interpersonal skills, problem-solving, information technology and modern languages. This programme would last two years, would be composed of many separate modules (which would be individually assessed) and would end with a final 'summative' assessment covering the work as a whole. The modules would be based on the existing National Certificate modules, and, like them, would be internally assessed by teachers. But the summative elements would be externally assessed. Students taking it would normally leave school at the end of fifth year, but it would be possible to start the programme in school and finish it in a further education college.

The other pathway would be called the Scottish Baccalaureate (Scotbac), modelled on the baccalauréat in France and other similar schemes in Denmark and elsewhere. It would be mainly academic in character, although with vocational elements, and would last for three years. There would be a core curriculum that would be common to all the variants, in particular between the broadly arts-based and the broadly science-based versions. Each variant would have a major subject that would be studied to a level that would be well beyond the existing Higher, and possibly also beyond the existing Sixth Year Studies courses. Nevertheless, the courses would be mostly based on existing Higher and SYS courses. There would be assessment at the end of each of the three years, but only the last one would be external: the first two years would be assessed by teachers themselves. The final external assessment would be summative, and would provide a group award in the programme as a whole: no longer would students have results in individual subjects. The committee estimated that about 40 per cent of students would take the Scotbac.

Howie tried to fend off what was to be the main point of controversy, the apparent divisiveness of having two tracks. A whole chapter of the report was devoted to the issue of how students could transfer between the tracks. Rather little was made of transfer from Scotbac to Scotcert, the report suggesting that this would be easy, and that people who had started on a predominantly academic course could readily catch up on the vocational elements of Scotcert. Lack of attention in the report to the practical difficulties this would entail in schools was a mistake. It tended to reinforce the idea that the Scotcert was not an intrinsically attractive option, because if transfer into it would be as straightforward as the report claimed, then its educational rationale could not have been as coherent as the report claimed. The rather bland reassurance about this direction of transfer also took no account of the weight of some of the research evidence that had come from the Centre for Educational Sociology – on how the option of falling back onto a safety net was one of the reasons why the Scottish system encouraged students to stay on beyond age 16. As we have seen, Howie's analysis had rejected this argument on the grounds that it was based on a widespread experience of failure, but Howie's recommendations on transfers from Scotbac to Scotcert had nothing to say about the presumably even more acute sense of failure that would come from dropping out of an entire programme (as opposed to just an individual course).

The crucial direction of transfer, however, was the other way, because its being realistically available depended on the capacity of the new scheme to encourage wider access to academic education in school and to university. The fear of the critics of this element of the proposal was that it would shut students out of university by age 15, and indeed even sooner since teachers would be anticipating students' likely choice of pathway as early as second year of secondary school. The report proposed that transfer would be easiest from the two general Scotcert tracks – arts and sciences – since students on these would already be acquiring some of the general education that would be at the heart of Scotbac. But there was no getting away from the point that the Scotbac was meant to be at a higher level intellectually, and so the report also had to propose 'summer bridging courses' to help students make the transition. There was no comment on the resources required for this – especially the resources of teacher time. The report peremptorily dismissed the likelihood of widespread transfer from the vocational Scotcert to Scotbac, 'because such students will have deliberately opted to take a vocational route'. This assumed a fixity of vocational aspirations that would never have been tenable at any time since the 1960s – research evidence showing that young people changed their minds frequently about their preferred careers in the last three years of secondary school – and was even more out of touch amidst the bewildering changes in the youth labour market that were engulfing not just Scotland but all developed countries. The absence of any representative of industry on the committee was perhaps most apparent in the naivety of its assumptions about students' entry into employment.

The report was also quite explicit about why it had rejected other routes for reform. It rejected A-levels because they were too narrow. It also rejected the adoption in Scotland of the International Baccalaureate, a worldwide system that is widely accepted for university entry: it was claimed that only a small minority of fifth- and sixth-year students in Scotland would be capable of attempting it. But the report reserved its main criticism for the option of wholesale modularisation of fifth and sixth year, an approach that was favoured by some of the evidence which the inquiry had received. The growing trend to modularisation was noted, not just in school but also in further and higher education. It was acknowledged that modularisation does offer many advantages: 'ease of access by students to individual components of courses; the accumulation of qualifications on a flexible basis over a number of years; ease of updating in response to technological and social change; the identification and provision of common elements in different courses; the motivation and clarity of purpose which can be engendered by short-term targets'.

But the committee did not feel that these strengths outweighed the disadvantages, and the summary they offered of these turned out to be prescient of what was to happen in the attempted reform in 1999–2000: 'Modularisation can lead to fragmentation and trivialisation of learning. It can also be associated with over-assessment and with assessment-driven learning. We realise, of course, that these problems can be overcome by imaginative course design which employs integration and linkage of modules.

However, it may be argued that if a course is intended almost exclusively to be delivered as an integrated whole to a stable class group, there is no reason to disintegrate it in the first place.'

What is more, modularisation necessitates an excessive reliance on internal assessment, because 'it is simply not feasible to assess externally so many small components'. The report claimed that the proposed Scotcert and Scotbac would be able to recognise 'partial student attainment' without the fragmentation entailed by full modularisation.

REACTIONS TO HOWIE

John Howie continued to take an active role in the debate in the latter part of 1992, indicating by then that his committee's proposals had to be interpreted flexibly. For example, in a speech in September 1992 to headteachers in north-east Scotland, he accepted that the committee should not have been so prescriptive about Scotbac being almost the sole route of entry to higher education. He also took every opportunity to emphasise that there was a consensus for change of some sort. He rejected the 'conspiracy theory' that the committee had been set up in order to anglicise Scottish education, and insisted that the proposals had to be seen as thoroughly European, distancing himself from the growing Euroscepticism in the Conservative government. To be European, he said, was to show 'courage and confidence' in the future.

He did this because the initial reaction to the report was very suspicious of the two tracks of Scotbac and Scotcert. The Labour Party education spokesman, Tony Worthington, for example, while not rejecting the idea outright, said that the main test would be whether Scotcert was of the same educational quality as Scotbac. The Conservatives' education spokeswoman, Astrid Ritchie, said she found the proposals exciting, but warned her colleagues not to be tempted into any reform that would resemble the English A-levels. The teachers' unions also were suspicious of potential anglicisation and of the twin-tracking, but their main objection was that Scottish education was already suffering from 'innovation fatigue', in the words of the general secretary of the

EIS. The general secretary of the smaller union, the Scottish Secondary Teachers Association, warned that teachers were rather cynical about utopian blueprints from university professors: 'Many teachers will reflect that they have heard it all before – Brunton, the Munn Report, the Dunning Report, et al. Some might well reflect that if the appointment of fresh committees to inquire into the problems of Scottish education could bring their solution, we should long ago have been living in an educational utopia.'

The educational leader of the local authorities, Strathclyde councillor Ian Davidson, warned that 'the last thing Scotland needs is a total reversal of everything that's gone before'.

The direction in which the weight of later comments would go was indicated early on (in June 1992) by Tom McCool, chief executive of the Vocational Education Council which ran the National Certificate modules. While welcoming the report's analysis and praising its boldness, he had this to say about the rejection of complete modularisation: 'The creation of "bridges" between the two routes, which will be vitally important in allaying concern on this issue, would have been assisted by the choice of a common modular structure for both routes.'

The written responses received by the committee were in remarkable agreement on most features of the report. Almost all accepted the critique of existing arrangements. The local authorities, for example, recorded 'general support for the analysis of the need for change'. The Association of Directors of Education in the local authorities accepted that 'the Howie Report argues clearly and cogently that aspects of the present system of upper secondary educational provision are unsatisfactory'. The Scottish Trades Union Congress said that Howie's strength was 'its substantial analysis and critique of the current arrangements'. The official response of Napier University was that the report contained 'a persuasive dissection of failings in the present system'. And the National Union of Students accepted 'that current provision of Highers are outmoded in relation to changes which have occurred around them, such as modularisation, the expansion of vocational elements in education and differentiation of certification levels in Standard Grade'.

The notable but almost isolated exception to this agreement

with Howie on his analysis was Andrew McPherson, in a public lecture upon receipt of a Fellowship from the Scottish Council for Research in Education in 1992. He denied that Scottish students suffered in higher education: there was, he said, no evidence that they are badly prepared, and substantial evidence that they do manage to find their feet when they get there. That evidence included, for example, a drop-out rate that was among the lowest in Europe, bettered only by the much more selective English university system. McPherson also reiterated the importance of the incremental structure of fifth and sixth year in encouraging staying-on beyond age 16. However, in the context of the general agreement with Howie, McPherson's assertion of the virtues of flexibility could readily be cited as evidence in favour of modularisation, and indeed that principle came to be the focus of much of the comment on Howie's proposals for Scotcert and Scotbac.

Responses agreed on eight problems with these, a weight of comment that was to prove irresistible to the inspectorate when it was drawing up its own proposals for reform after the consultation period on Howie was over.

The first was the twin-tracking itself, which was widely seen as divisive. For example, the Scottish Consultative Council on the Curriculum – the government's own curriculum advisers – argued that the twin-track idea 'will be to the detriment of the majority of young people without being significantly to the benefit of any'. The STUC summed up the very widespread view that the proposals 'would completely undermine Scottish comprehensive education, by creating a two-tier system'. The EIS described twin-tracking as 'the basic fault in Howie'. The directors of education regarded twin-tracking as 'divisive and élitist'. It could, they said, 'undermine the principles of equality of opportunity integral to the continuation of a coherent and comprehensive education system'. The Scottish Chambers of Commerce – which had not wanted any change at all – said the proposals 'would not resolve the problems of the latter stages of education'.

Part of the reason for these doubts about the twin tracks was a scepticism that transfer between them would be feasible in practice – the second objection. Richard Watt, the depute headteacher of Penicuik High School, put it graphically to a conference of the Scottish Association for Educational Management and Administration: 'It is more like snakes and ladders where it becomes easier to slide down from Scotbac to Scotcert than the reverse. This is particularly true for the sciences where a body of knowledge has to be acquired first.'

That would be a problem because Scotbac would in practice be bound to be of higher esteem socially than Scotcert, the third objection. You could not legislate away centuries of a highly academic education system in which academic ability was venerated. The Scottish Parent Teacher Council put this well, arguing that 'parity of esteem' between Scotcert and Scotbac would be impossible to achieve, and that most parents would push their children into Scotbac even though they were not able to cope with the demands that would then be placed on them.

The fourth objection was that only large schools could afford to offer all subjects, especially in Scotbac. As Andrew McPherson had pointed out earlier, this would cause severe problems for rural schools and schools in working-class areas. Tayside Regional Council – which governed education in both urban Dundee and Perth and rural Perthshire and Angus – estimated the effects on staffing and school organisation of the reforms, and concluded that, without a massive increase in resources, 'smaller secondary schools, particularly those in rural areas, would be seriously disadvantaged'. In the extreme case, there could be a slow reintroduction of two kinds of secondary school in Scotland, specialising in either Scotbac or Scotcert, but not both – a return to selection by another name, as Gerry Docherty, the depute rector of Grangemouth High School put it. Margaret Alcorn, the assistant head of Castlebrae High School in the Craigmillar district of Edinburgh, predicted that 'the bigger schools will get bigger, and the smaller schools, especially in the peripheral housing schemes, will die'.

The fifth objection was to one of Howie's proposed ways of dealing with this problem of small schools. The report had suggested that schools could form consortia among themselves or with further education colleges. The critics said this would be difficult to operate, especially outwith the urban areas, and also ignored the different educational traditions of the two sectors. Schools were predominantly academic, colleges predominantly vocational. In any case, the Conservative government was in the process of removing the colleges from the control of local authorities, and so amicable working relationships with schools would become more difficult (and costly).

Sixth, there were widespread doubts about the moving of Standard Grade to third year. The Curriculum Council pointed out that the committee had not cited hard evidence that there was any problem with the pace of learning in the first three years of secondary – it had all come from one source, the inspectorate – and said that the new curriculum for ages 5–14 that was still being put in place would be a better way of dealing with any difficulties. In any case, the arguments which Howie gave for moving Standard Grade were actually better expressed as arguments for its abolition: if it was not a leaving exam (as it could not be at age 15), why have it at all?

The seventh argument concerned higher education. It was feared that the intention that Scotbac should reach more advanced levels of academic achievement than were currently available in schools would threaten the four-year honours degree in Scottish universities. The greater rigidity of the Scotbac and Scotcert structure would, it was feared, lead to a reduction in the proportion of young people who qualified to enter university.

The eighth and last objection may seem to be the most mundane but in an era of tight public finances may have been one of the most telling. It was pointed out that the Howie committee had had no remit for implementation – no requirement to report on how a new scheme could be managed, or paid for, or staffed. This objection did not come only from teacher unions, concerned that their members had already been working through too many innovations in the previous decade – Standard Grade, the National Certificate, the 5–14 curriculum, along with a host of disparate other initiatives such as on vocational education. Indeed, the EIS itself went far beyond these in its comments on the resource implications: 'The EIS does not share the naïve belief of the Howie committee that a major innovation can be introduced

for no greater cost than a little staff development and some central
support for curriculum development.'

It was also pointed out by local authorities and others that any
reform as radical as Howie proposed would require extensive staff
training, new accommodation to allow the full range of courses to
be provided, new computer hardware and software to administer
the new courses (especially any growth in internal assessment),
new facilities for offering vocational education in schools (since
that had been the province of the colleges), and new costs if that
did indeed encourage more students to stay on at school. It was
also suggested that any new system would require massive
investment in the costs of examining and certification – another
prescient point when seen from the aftermath of what happened
in 2000. This was a point made by the specialist-subject panels of
the Examination Board, although was not emphasised either by
the board or by the Vocational Education Council in their submissions. The EIS commented that extensive moderation would be
required to maintain standards of internal assessment (that is,
regular checks of teachers' marking standards by representatives
of the examining body). This, the union said, would be required
to be funded at a sufficiently generous level 'as to permit the
implementation without stress to either schools or individual
teachers'.

CONCLUSIONS
It has been worth looking at the Howie committee in detail
because it was the moment at which reform of the Highers became
inevitable. Even though a case for the merely incremental
modification of the status quo had been made by Professor
Andrew McPherson, the sheer weight of contrary opinion made
change unstoppable. The Conservative government that was in an
embattled minority position in Scotland – still able to command
no more than a quarter of the vote in the 1992 general election
that closely followed upon the report of the committee – was
never likely to go to the barricades over something which seemed
to have little to do with its own core ideology. Reform of the
Highers was not like, say, the privatising of nationalised

industries, or even like the emerging Conservative idea of forcing schools out of local-authority control. How an exam system was organised seemed to be largely a technical matter.

The Howie report also inadvertently influenced the character of the change that subsequently came about. As McPherson had noted, there was really only one option that was not the status quo and not the tracked system that was common in the rest of Europe: modularisation. That was what the comments on Howie concentrated on – 'an evolutionary scheme based on a single award', according to the local authorities; a wholly 'unitised' (in other words modularised) system according to the EIS; 'a staged modular course' in the view of the Scottish Parent Teacher Council. The Scottish Higher Education Funding Council described the rejection of full modularisation as regrettable, and 'flying in the face of developments in the rest of the education system'. As we will see in the next chapter, this is exactly how the inspectorate chose to take the pressure for reform forward, with the ultimate outcome in Higher Still.

Nevertheless, although leaving the reform to drift with the consensus may have been politically inevitable, it did leave what eventually emerged lacking in any coherent statement of educational rationale. The details of that are for the next chapter. What we can take from the evidence and arguments surrounding Howie is that Scottish education was still being powered by the principles and ideologies that had come to dominate it in the 1960s. Comprehensive schooling was sacrosanct, equality of opportunity was the guiding aim, and a continuing urge to modernise was widely accepted. Allegations of dwelling in the mythological past were coming to be one of the most effective rhetorical accusations that could be levelled at defenders of Scottish culture and Scottish education.

What was lacking in these important organisational and political principles was the kind of concern with the cultural purpose of education that had motivated many previous inquiries right back to the foundation of the Highers themselves. Just one example can illustrate it. The entire spectrum of comment on Howie accepted uncritically the report's brief reassertion of the principle of curricular breadth (which was quoted above). Nowhere, either in the report or in the comment, was there a discussion of what breadth might be, philosophically or educationally. It was equated quite simply with students doing lots of types of courses, which can at best be described as a principle of management. Breadth could then quite readily be associated with modularisation.

The final conclusion from this chapter is that the one body that got its way in all this was the schools inspectorate. As we have seen in the previous chapter, it had been pressing for a change to the fifth and sixth year for many decades, and it finally got its inquiry almost by the accident of the misfortunes of the Scottish Conservative Party. The inspectorate was in charge of the Howie debate, through its briefing papers and statistics, through its role as assessors to the committee and through its commissioning of research into some aspects of the debates – for example, research into drop-out rates in higher education, but not into the funding and social rationale for expanding higher education. Andrew McPherson pointed out, in his SCRE lecture in 1992, that in some crucial respects the inspectorate actually misrepresented unpublished research conclusions to the committee, notably over the chances of success at university of Scottish students who were gaining just enough Highers to enter. McPherson's conclusions on the inspectors' role are worth quoting in full: 'It is inevitable that the makers of policy will attempt to manage and control both the creative and the subversive elements of the research contribution. We see the effects of this management, or mismanagement, at its worst in the abuse of research that Howie represents. More fundamentally, we must question the whole organisation through which Howie collated, assimilated and reproduced the ideas and the products of research in producing its tendentious account.'

The consensual acceptance of Howie's critique opened the way to reform, and the rejection of Howie's proposals passed the initiative on the nature of reform back to the inspectors. Never before had they been presented with such an unambiguously popular opportunity to determine the very character of a key part of Scottish education.

CHAPTER 4

Higher Still

The outcome of the debate about Howie's proposals seemed to be fairly clear. The status quo was widely accepted as not being an option, but so also were Howie's proposals for separate tracks. So overwhelming was the consensus of criticism of tracking that there was quickly no point in questioning it: the Howie proposals were dead by the end of 1992. Into the vacuum thus created stepped the inspectorate, coming up with its own response to Howie's criticism of the Highers and to the education community's criticism of Howie. The inspectorate proposals were made policy, and became in due course the Higher Still reform that was put in place in 2000.

Looking back, that all now seems fairly inevitable. The debate seemed destined to turn out the way it did, and so the disaster of 2000 seemed fated to happen. But was it? And was the inspectorate solely responsible? After all, wasn't it simply articulating a consensus? Did Scottish education truly subscribe to the principles of Higher Still? Did the consensus that seemed, by 1999, to be in place around it really run deep? Answering these questions will get to the heart of the wider questions which this reform can teach us about how to make policy and how something as complex as an examination system can be reformed.

OPPORTUNITY FOR ALL?
The document which launched the process of reform was issued by Ian Lang, Secretary of State for Scotland, on 3 March 1994. Its full title was *Higher Still: Opportunity for All*. The first part of that, which came to be the shorthand name for the whole reform, was a rather dreadful pun, in keeping with the style which the post-1992 Conservative government seemed to favour. (Another example was its response to the pressure for a Scottish parliament

with 'Scotland in the Union: a Partnership for Good'.) It was as if it believed that it could fend off deep political hostility to its régime by merely asserting that what it was proposing would be a continuation of Scottish traditions – here insisting that it was not in the business of abolishing the Highers and replacing them with A-levels – while at the same time aiming for ever-higher standards in education. The subtitle was conceived in similar vein, attempting to appeal to the evident Scottish support for equal opportunities by appearing to offer an assessment system that would cater for all levels of ability.

The document accepted the criticisms of existing arrangements which Howie had set out, referring to them as 'a penetrating analysis of the problems in the current system', but noted two main objections to the proposals. One was on twin-tracking. The other was on the idea of moving Standard Grade to third year. This latter may seem to be a rather minor feature to have singled out, and it certainly did not feature nearly so prominently in the submissions on Howie as other comments, but it was crucial to how the inspectorate wanted to move forward. If there were not to be three school years following Standard Grade, as Howie proposed, then we were back to the two-year period over which there had been stalemate in the discussions leading up to Howie.

The Higher Still proposals contained seven key features, all presented as no more than 'evolutionary change' from the existing system. The first, politically potent, point was that the Highers would remain but would be extended. It was revealing that the authors of the document chose to present a new Advanced Higher as the first aspect of reform, 'to set a clear and demanding benchmark for more able students'. Able students would bypass Highers and take Advanced courses over two years. Moreover, the most academically able students would be encouraged to use a good clutch of Advanced Higher passes to enter directly into the second year of university courses. Starting with the Advanced Higher in this way seems to sit awkwardly with the subtitle of the document ('opportunity for all'), with the concerns about the excessively academic character of Howie's Scotbac, and with the long-running worries that the Highers would be replaced by A-levels. But that last puzzle is precisely the point. Here, finally, was the opportunity that the inspectorate had been looking for over a period of 40 years – the opportunity to introduce an A-level-type exam which could be presented as part of a democratising package that would be in keeping with Scottish traditions. Mentioning the Advanced Higher first was, in that historical view, no accident.

Second, in other respects the Higher would remain in place, including the option of sitting it in either fifth or sixth year. But in one respect it, too, would change. Both it and the Advanced Higher would be turned into modules, and these would be drawn from an amalgamation of the courses issuing from the Examination Board and those that were part of the vocational National Certificate administered by the Vocational Education Council. Most modules would last for 40 hours, there would be four in a Higher course, and so the total length of a Higher course would rise by about 40 hours in an attempt to answer the criticism that the Highers were not deep enough. As between courses, however, Howie's planned coherence was abandoned: 'students should be able to take a mix of courses as best suits their aptitudes and aspirations'. In case that looked like complete freedom of choice, the document also said that 'it will be important that students' programmes are coherent, have clear progression and display suitable breadth'. How schools and colleges could judge that would be the subject of centrally issued 'guidelines'.

Third (but only third) the proposals talked about 'a unified system of courses and assessment'; this was where the subtitle was supposed to be most relevant. Although this idea of unifying academic and vocational courses was later cited as one of the main features of the system – and held up as Scotland taking a lead in Europe – such philosophical issues were not given any prominence in the document. A unified framework was needed to give National Certificate modules the same standing as Highers and Advanced Highers. This would, it was claimed, 'improve continuity and progression' for people moving between academic and vocational courses, encourage 'parity of esteem' between such courses, and create a system of qualifications that would be easier to understand and simpler to administer.

Fourth, these new courses would be offered at three levels below Higher, giving five levels altogether, thus taking forward the principle of differentiating levels that had been put in place for Standard Grade in fourth year. Although it was not proposed 'at this time' that courses would be grouped together into bundles with particular titles, the limits on the Scottish Office's policy-making autonomy were clear in the retention of the fairly new General Scottish Vocational Qualifications, which were being developed as the Scottish contribution to the British government's policy on vocational training. GSVQs were made up of suites of National Certificate modules, and were precisely group awards. So there was to be grouping for vocational courses, but not for academic ones.

Fifth, despite the general abandonment of Howie's idea of moving Standard Grade to third year, able students would be encouraged to do so. This became known as 'fast-tracking'.

There was also, sixth, an unequivocal statement on assessment. It would be 'criterion-based', which, as we saw in Chapter 3, was based on the idea that students should be judged on whether their attainment had met certain criteria, not on how they performed in comparison to other students. There was little indication, though, of whether that criterion-referencing would be based on the 'competences' that had come to dominate assessment in vocational education, or on older-established principles of examining students' understanding of a body of knowledge laid down in a syllabus as had been retained in Standard Grade even while also shifting to criterion-referencing.

It was also made clear that, as in the vocational assessments, internal testing would be a key part of the programme, although external assessment would also be used because it would be more reliable, more credible to the public, and less of an imposition on teachers and lecturers. Because of the greater use of internal assessment, there would also have to be a system of 'moderation', by which the examining body would periodically check teachers' own marking standards.

The seventh and final aspect of the proposals was that all students should demonstrate that they possessed certain 'core skills', which were rather arbitrarily (and with dubious syntax) listed as 'the five core skills: communication, numeracy, information technology, problem-solving, and personal and interpersonal skills'. The last of these became 'personal effectiveness' during the development of Higher Still.

For what would turn out to be an enormous upheaval, the government was obdurately insistent that little was actually changing. Ian Lang said that 'ministers believe that, by building on existing courses, they will not impose additional burdens on teachers'. This became a key theme in attempts to reconcile teachers to the reforms – that the changes were only in assessment, not in courses. What was taught and learned would simply be reorganised into new, modular units, at five levels. It was not a change to the curriculum.

Immediate reaction was much more positive than it had been to Howie's proposals. An editorial in the *Times Educational Supplement Scotland* – the influential and authoritative weekly newspaper of Scottish education – mentioned three strengths. Because Higher Still would unify academic and vocational systems, and because it would be modular, it would not be as divisive as Howie's twin-tracking. It was an amendment to fifth and sixth years rather than a revolution. And it was the final piece in a thought-through system of progression from early primary to the end of secondary (building on Standard Grade and on the curriculum for ages 5–14). Only the retention of General Scottish Vocational Qualifications was criticised as being inimical to the flexibility that the rest of the package seemed to offer. The paper was pessimistic about success, however, because of 'stubborn conservatism in the form of teachers whose idealism and zeal for reform have been exhausted in introducing Standard Grade'.

Professor Howie himself had more serious reservations, seeing the proposals as disappointingly cautious. He did not believe that twin-tracking had been avoided, since in practice students would be likely to assemble modules that looked like his Scotcert or Scotbac anyway. That ad hoc assemblage would lack the planned coherence that Howie had wanted to give his pathways. But after expressing these initial reservations, he largely withdrew from the debate, leaving the field to the less severe criticisms that came from other people.

The main worries were expressed by teachers' representatives. The EIS objected to fast-tracking in Standard Grade, saying this would create new divides between academic and vocational study when Higher Still was attempting to end them. They said that lengthening the Higher course to 160 hours would inevitably lead to students taking fewer Highers, and so to a narrowing of the overall curriculum. And they spotted that the Advanced Highers looked very like A-levels, and could undermine the entire idea of breadth in school and higher education, and would bring into question the four-year university degree. But the most politically telling point from the unions was on the scale of the upheaval. The general secretary of the EIS, Jim Martin, warned that 'for Ian Lang glibly to suggest that this is simply an extension of existing courses is laughable', and Alan Lamont, his counterpart in the Scottish Secondary Teachers Association, believed that 'teachers are not going to be conned into doing what they did for Standard Grade when they were told the same story and suddenly found themselves in the midst of a huge development programme which imposed horrendous burdens on them'.

Both unions pointed out that the new money that Mr Lang had promised covered only the development programme – the technical aspects of devising new arrangements for assessment, for example. There was nothing for extra teachers, or for extra administrative support in schools. This worried the unions because a massive increase in internal assessment would hugely increase schools' administrative burden.

But the broad welcome encouraged the inspectorate to go ahead. The immediate concerns did not go away, but they could be ignored because the basic idea of Higher Still seemed to be building on the consensus in the responses to Howie. It was easy to go ahead also because this entire reform required almost no new legislation. The new courses and assessment, the amalgamation of academic and vocational programmes, the change in assessment principles: these were all completely under the control of civil servants, inspectors, quangos, and schools. Legislation was required only on what appeared to be the relatively minor matter of whether there should continue to be two examining bodies – the Examination Board and the Vocational Education Council. The government consulted on this, found another consensus, favouring a merger, legislated for it in 1996, and set up a new Scottish Qualifications Authority which took over the old exams and modules on 1 April 1997, two years before the new exams came on stream.

For the much more difficult administrative business of actually pushing forward the detailed reforms, the government established a Higher Still Development Unit, headed by Mary Pirie, who had a background in vocational education and management training in schools in Lothian. This unit was, in effect, an outstation of the inspectorate, as was made clear by the head of the inspectorate when he appeared before the parliamentary inquiry on 9 October 2000, referring also to the role of the relevant chief inspector, Philip Banks, and Eleanor Emberson, civil service head of the curriculum group within the Education Department: 'The head of the Higher Still Development Unit works to Philip Banks in pure line management terms. He is responsible for agreeing with her the targets that she will meet and for discussing with her the delivery of those targets. The Higher Still Development Unit is managed by a body called the Development Unit Advisory Group, which is chaired by a colleague from within the department, Eleanor Emberson.'

Ms Pirie announced that her job was 'setting the framework and taking away the panic'. As the *Times Educational Supplement Scotland* pointed out, 'All [her] previous postings were in sensitive areas, not calculated to endear anyone to a weary and over-managed profession'. She responded by promising to develop 'a relationship of openness and trust'. She also promised 'brief, concise and accessible documentation', and not to impose 'a Canadian forest on people'.

A rather more dismaying impression was created by one trivial matter near the beginning of the Higher Still Development Unit's work. Continuing with the punning title of the reform, it adopted as its logo a sort of stylised mountain range, a bit like a bar of

Toblerone chocolate, presumably to demonstrate that they intended to take us to alpine heights. Such meretriciousness does not go down well in Scottish education. An already rather cynical teaching profession was inclined to see this minor detail as indicating yet another triumph of presentation over substance.

GROWING CONCERNS

The odd thing about what then happened over the following four years was how ineffective the combination of inspectorate and Development Unit was in allaying initial and growing concerns. Probably the high point of the consensus was in fact the moment at which the Higher Still document was published, because the relief at not getting Howie's proposals was so great. The puzzle is why those who were leading the development of the policy failed to capitalise on this goodwill. Usually the process is the reverse: initial criticisms fade away as the reality of having to implement reforms looms. That happened with Standard Grade, where the eventual outcome was actually further from the consensual view than the original Munn and Dunning reports had been in 1977. It happened with comprehensive schooling, where the controversies of the 1960s had more or less been forgotten in Scotland by the late 1970s. But it did not happen with Higher Still, where disputes continued to undermine morale and momentum.

It is possible to pick out three educational concerns which were expressed from the start and which seem to have lasting significance now that Higher Still is in place; a further five emerged as the development progressed. The first of the three was simply timescale. The original target set for starting the new courses was summer 1997. This was probably never realistic, and was relaxed twice, first for one year in August 1995 when Michael Forsyth became Secretary of State for Scotland, and then again for a further year by Brian Wilson, the Scottish education minister in the new Labour government. Repeated assurances that the timetable was achievable simply did not persuade teachers. For example, there was deep scepticism when Nisbet Gallacher, then head of the inspectorate, claimed in April 1994 that the development programme would not affect teachers 'very significantly'. By November of that year, the chief inspector in charge of Higher Still, Ron Tuck, had had to shift away from that position and admit that 'there is a danger in overemphasising minimum change. Minimum change in particular areas may mean significant change and we're not trying to con anyone.' (Mr Tuck later became chief executive of the Scottish Qualifications Authority.) But that was not seen as a reason to delay. Mr Gallacher, in May 1995, even suggested to the Headteachers Association of Scotland that 'if this were an audience of, say, businessmen, they might think that two years was a fairly generous timescale'. That did not go down well. It appears, in fact, that each delay was achieved by political intervention from ministers: this is how Mr Forsyth's delay was reported by the *Times Educational Supplement Scotland*, and that was never denied. The ambition (some would say hubris) of the inspectors was reluctant to accept such political interference.

The other two persisting concerns were a residue of the debate around Howie. The second worry was over fast-tracking. It was argued (for example, by Brian Boyd, a lecturer at Jordanhill College of Education, and former headteacher) that this threatened the very principles of comprehensive education, especially when combined with a new attainment level in the curriculum for ages 5–14. In an article in September 1995, he said that the people in overall charge of the reform lacked vision, especially any understanding of how the Scottish comprehensive system worked. Although Dr Boyd and others praised the explicit attention in the programme to children with special educational needs, there were misgivings that, without substantial extra resources, schools could not possibly give such students real extra choice. One teacher was quoted in the *Times Educational Supplement Scotland* in December 1995 as saying that the proposals for such students were fine in principle but impossible in practice: 'Many of the people who come up with these kinds of proposals are lecturers and others who are so removed from the daily grind that what they spout is totally unrealistic.'

Related to this concern were persisting reservations about the implications of the Advanced Higher, the third matter. These worries tended to be dismissed as not of fundamental importance. For example, Frank Pignatelli, a member of the strategy group that was charged with overseeing the implementation, and director of education in Strathclyde Region, said in September 1995 that the issue of the status of the Advanced Higher in gaining entry to university was of importance only for what he called 'the high-fliers', and was much narrower than 'the aims of Higher Still'. What was never publicly acknowledged was that, as participation in higher education began to approach one half of all young people, the structure of university courses could no longer be described as being of concern only to an academic élite. If the Advanced Higher really did lead to a reduction of the Scottish honours degree to three years, at least in some institutions, then that would truly disadvantage precisely those candidates of middling academic ability who formed the bulk of the new clientele of the universities.

These worries about the narrowing implications of Advanced Higher for schools remained. A meeting of headteachers in December 1995 feared that the Advanced Higher would be less demanding than the existing Certificate of Sixth Year Studies and yet would lead to a narrowing of choice because of the lengthening of the course. This concern was exacerbated when the SQA announced in March 1998 that Advanced Highers were equivalent in demand to A-levels. The distinctiveness of the Scottish fifth and sixth years seemed under threat.

There were consequential worries about the effects on breadth of study in higher education. At the annual meeting of the Committee of Scottish Higher Educational Principals in November 1994, several concerns were expressed that the Advanced Higher would encourage direct entry to second year, thus denying students the potentially broadening first-year experience of studying one or two subjects beyond their main specialisms. And the concerns over the implications for course length in higher education were exacerbated after the publication of the Scottish section of the Dearing report on Higher Education in July 1997. That recommended a growth in three-year degrees, ostensibly as a means of reinvigorating the breadth of the old Scottish Ordinary degree, but also under pressure to save money. For honours degrees, it noted that 'the new Advanced Highers are liable to overlap with the first year of the higher education curriculum', and so entry into second year should be feasible, possibly after some sort of 'bridging programme' during the year between school and university. On the other hand, amongst those who favoured this and admired the Advanced Higher, there was a resurrection of Howie's criticism of the Highers as offering inadequate preparation for higher education. For example, Keir Bloomer, director of education in Clackmannanshire, argued in August 1997 that the whole debate since Howie had been evading difficult issues like this one: 'A sixth year of genteel idleness is hardly the best preparation for higher education or later life.'

Another five educational concerns were absent at the beginning in 1994 but grew in significance as the reality of the reforms became clearer. The first was the hoary old issue of modularisation. Most did not worry about it initially: it had, after all, been a key feature of the consensus around Howie. But the practicability and potential of it came increasingly to be doubted. Partly that was a matter of excessive assessment, a point to which we will return in a moment, and partly it had to do with the integrity of some courses, notably English, an example which will be discussed at length later in this chapter. But the general concern was simply about the anarchy of choice. There was a proposal for a new set of Scottish Group Awards, intended to recognise breadth of study. The groups would indeed enforce some breadth, rather in the manner recognised by Howie, but the essentially modular character of the Higher Still reform might tend to undermine them. If there was no incentive to students to seek a group award, young people might wonder why they should bother, citing the rhetoric of choice that surrounded the whole Higher Still debate. Students would not be interested in studying for a group award unless the award actually had value. For example, in the words of Charles Smith, rector of Airdrie Academy, writing in December 1996, 'The universities should give currency to the group award.'

The second worry was about so-called 'multi-level' teaching. This had arisen ultimately because there was a severe limitation on the resources that would be available for implementing the programme. So, with five levels in Higher Still (a number that did not vary, even though their character and naming did), teachers would find themselves teaching, in the same class and at the same time, students who were aiming for quite different qualifications. That might just about work if the syllabuses of the two courses were the same, but in some subjects that was not the case: for example, in geography by 1999 the syllabuses for the Higher course and for the next level down (Intermediate 2) contained large elements that were incompatible. In all subjects there were some combinations of students who would never be compatible because of their different levels of ability, and yet, in a small school, there would simply not be enough teachers in minority subjects (which is most subjects apart from English and mathematics) to hold more than one class at the fifth-year level. The educational implications of multi-level teaching were so serious that, by late 1996 and early 1997, they became one of the main reasons why further delays in implementing Higher Still were being recommended by such powerful bodies as the Headteachers Association and the Association of Directors of Education. As we have seen, there was a further postponement, but the official response was typically that expressed in a letter to every secondary headteacher from Brian Wilson's successor as education minister, Helen Liddell, in September 1998: 'No school will be expected or need to provide all subjects at all levels' – which can hardly have been reassuring to teachers who took literally the Higher Still slogan of opportunity for all. 'And,' she continued, 'schools may wish to consider other options for small groups [of students] such as inter-school or school-college partnerships,' proposals that, as we saw in the previous chapter, were rejected as largely impracticable when they were made by the Howie committee.

The third concern was related to that, and was about internal assessment. As the paperwork started to flood out of the Development Unit and later the SQA, it became evident that internal assessment would impose enormous burdens on schools. By the time the first courses were running, the SQA had issued around nine million sheets of A4 paper advising on assessment.

If they hadn't also offered schools the option of CD-Roms from which they could print out their own copies, they would have had to have issued some 77 million sheets. Mary Pirie's aspiration to save the Canadian forests seemed to be going up in flames, as was Ian Lang's and Nisbet Gallacher's intention not to affect teachers 'significantly'. Not that anyone had really believed these assurances at the start. As George Haggarty, headteacher of St John's High School in Dundee, had warned in May 1994, 'Instead of assessment for all, it's assessment all of the time' – a point that, as we have seen, Howie's report itself recognised as the main drawback of modularisation. But what was changing from about late 1996 onwards was the realisation of what this meant in practice. For example, a meeting of teachers in North Ayrshire in November 1996 was concerned that students and teachers would have to spend too much time on assessment. The mere recording of results would be burdensome, they agreed, but more serious would be the intrusion of assessment on time that would be better spent on learning. In the words of George MacBride, the respected education convener of the EIS and a teacher in Govan, speaking to the *Times Educational Supplement Scotland* in December 1996: 'If you ask young people in fourth year if they're enjoying internal assessment, the answer is not exactly enthusiastic. The question has to be raised why we need quite so much certification and what are the benefits of this amount of certification to young people.'

The fourth objection to what was emerging concerned the curriculum. Issues were raised in many subjects, partly because there turned out in practice to be much more curricular change than had been forecast at the beginning. By December 1998, 11 of the 32 subjects at Higher level were scheduled to have a larger than 15 per cent change, most of them high-profile: accounting, art and design, chemistry, computing, English, home economics, modern studies, physical education, physics, religious studies, and secretarial studies. With the exception of home economics and religious studies, each of these was taken by several thousand students each year, and English was the most popular subject of all, with around 35,000 candidates annually. In the next section, we look at three specific subjects in more detail, and illustrate some of these curricular worries more fully.

Teachers felt, fifth, that there was a lack of a coherent educational philosophy in Higher Still. The most eloquent statement of the general point came later, from the Association of Directors of Education in their submission to one of the parliamentary inquiries into the exams crisis. They went right back to the origins of Higher Still, and pointed to the philistinism of the entire programme of development: 'The decision to create a unified academic and vocational qualification system produced many fundamentally conflicting views and interests which could only have been reconciled through consultation on issues of philosophy, purpose and overall design. Consultation focused instead on mechanistic, instrumental issues relating to implementation.'

We will return to a fuller discussion of the inquiries in Chapter 6; in particular, we will return to this submission because it shows the directors of education bidding to fill a vacuum in educational leadership in Scotland at a time when the very role of local authorities in education is being questioned. For the present, the point is that this view had been expressed with increasing urgency at least as far back as 1995. In July of that year, Willis Pickard, the editor of the *Times Educational Supplement Scotland*, used a review of a book by Richard Pring, the Oxford philosopher of education, to encourage the Higher Still programme to face up to 'the intellectually demanding task of combining liberal general education and vocational preparation'. In March 1996, likewise, the director of education in Glasgow, Ken Corsar, called for the reform to be delayed because it was not being given enough time to be developed coherently.

That makes eight groups of educational objections to Higher Still. Three were there from the start in 1994: the allegedly unrealistic timescale for implementation, various perceived threats to comprehensive education, and the threat which the proposed Advanced Higher allegedly posed to breadth of study at both school and university. A further five concerns grew as the programme developed: the practical difficulties of modularisation, the difficulties of multi-level teaching (students following different courses in the same classroom), worries about excessive assessment, the large and sometimes controversial changes being proposed in some parts of the curriculum (despite initial assurances that curricular changes would be minimal), and the lack of an overarching philosophy for the whole enterprise. The sustained nature of these educational objections shows that teachers and other educationalists had been engaging with the educational arguments around the reform for many years before the courses started in 1999. Teachers' resistance to change was largely based on well-argued educational grounds, not on the 'stubborn conservatism' of which they were accused in 1994.

PARTICULAR CURRICULAR SUBJECTS

Many of the eight areas of concern can be illustrated by considering three subjects in more depth. In two of these – computing and English – discussions about the curriculum and assessment became acrimonious, especially because teachers felt increasingly frustrated at not being consulted properly. A slightly different type of concern arose with the first exam in Higher Still mathematics in 2000 – about the philosophy of assessment rather than the curriculum.

Take computing first, where 20 per cent of the syllabus had changed, including 40 per cent of the work on software development. In a letter to the *Times Educational Supplement Scotland* in June 1998, a strong indictment of the new syllabus was given by four very senior educationalists: Tom Conlon, SQA principal examiner for SYS computing and a lecturer in the subject at Moray House College of Education; Lewis Smith, SQA principal examiner for Higher Grade computing and computing manager at George Watson's school in Edinburgh; Catriona McInnes, who had resigned in protest from the group which had been developing Higher Still computing and who had been awarded an MBE for services to computing in schools; and Peter Lennon, principal examiner designate for Higher Still computing. In other words, a group with impressive credentials. They had this to say about the Higher Still computing and information technology framework: 'The development now appears to be increasingly isolated from professional opinion. Recent "training days" [for teachers] have presented materials of uneven quality and completeness, and basic problems relating to assessment, multi-level teaching and IT resourcing remain unsolved.'

They went on to say that, properly taught, computing offers students 'an intellectual adventure in which new science and technology become the basis for exploring new forms of communication, problem-solving and creativity', but that 'in its present form Higher Still will not fulfil this promise, not only because it lacks any vision of computing beyond the mundane and vocational, but also because classroom teachers will struggle to overcome the mediocrity of the learning experience which the new courses imply'.

These are clearly not the words of people who are unconcerned with high academic standards, and earlier in their letter they also say that they share the Higher Still philosophy of wanting to extend these standards to 'a broad range of learners'. Such concerns had been raised as long ago as November 1995, when the specialist panel that advised the Examination Board on computing studies feared that speed was overtaking quality. Similar views were expressed in the same month at a conference in Edinburgh of computing studies teachers from all over Scotland. But the Development Unit pressed on, claiming that there was overwhelming support for their proposals.

The controversies in English were more spectacular than in any other area. This example matters particularly, not only because of the fact that English is taken by more students than any other subject, but also because of the role which English has played in Scottish education since the early twentieth century, as we saw in Chapter 2. The anger was summed up in the *Times Educational Supplement Scotland* in November 1995 by Elizabeth Leghorn, who was the principal teacher of English in Dingwall Academy: 'It is difficult to shake off the conviction that an educational philosophy which has for years underpinned Higher English has been holed below the water-line. The justification for the study of English is now the development of the "components of communicative competence" and "skills for personal and social development". Whatever happened to the ideals of the kindling of intellectual interests, the awakening of criticism and questioning, and the belief, to quote the Standard Grade arrangements, that "literature should be read and studied for its own sake"?'

These comments were made on the original proposals that came out from the committee which was developing the courses in the new subject that was to be called 'English and Communication'. Some of the concerns were organisational, notably, that the Higher Still Development Unit was issuing obscure, lengthy and badly written documents in which important issues of principle – such as the growth in internal assessment – were buried in a mass of technical and bureaucratic detail. In autumn 1997, for example, one set of documentation amounted to 300 pages of reading. There was resentment caused by a perception that the development was being led by people who were not qualified to do so: for example, only two of the 22 members of the development committee were practising English teachers.

There was a reiteration of the general concerns about resources. For example, the Development Unit material that teachers were supposed to use for the part of the course that dealt with report-writing amounted to 50 pages, which would have cost £1 per pupil to photocopy. So this one item could have cost over a third of the entire annual photocopying budget that the English department would have available for the Higher class. There was felt to be a threat to the autonomy of teachers in the system of national assessments drawn from a single national bank: such centrally devised tests could not possibly deal with all the literary texts that a teacher might want to use with a class, and the teachers would be forced to use only those books, poems and so on for which a test had been provided.

But the main concerns were about the content of the syllabus and the arrangements for examination. Two broad issues were raised in a paper prepared in autumn 1997 by a voluntary group of English teachers in Lothian. One was with the unmanageability of the assessment requirements – the familiar worry that the sheer volume of internal assessment would overwhelm teachers and students. It was feared that so much time would be spent on assessing that there would be sharply reduced opportunities for teaching and learning. This would especially be a problem if many students had to resit the internal assessments. A lengthy written response by the Development Unit in late autumn 1997 – claiming that, in practice, the amount of assessment would be no greater than in existing courses – was widely perceived as missing the point because it ignored the change in assessment style. In the old style of Higher, the assessments were under the control of the teacher, and were used in a formative way: detecting a student's strengths and weaknesses so that they could be given help in the most effective way possible. That type of assessment was not intrusive on good teaching, but was an integral part of it. The Higher Still assessments were for an external purpose, even though they were conducted by teachers. In the words of one prominent activist among the English teachers, John Aberdein of Stromness Academy, 'When the results of assessment are crucial to the academic and working career of a student, then a separation of roles between teacher and assessor is crucial. The teacher's role is educative, critical, supportive, holistic: not terminal.' These concerns would have had echoes among teachers of many subjects, not just English.

Even more worrying was the allegation that the new English courses were intellectually impoverished, reducing education to mere 'training'. These objections pointed out that the whole Higher Still reform had started with an assessment system, and that this had then forced a modification in what students had to learn, despite the initial assurances that the curriculum would not change. The 'communications' element of the title of the course, it was feared, had come to dominate. This was often expressed as a perception that the Vocational Education Council's approach had taken over: instead of English being about the study and discussion of literature, it was being reduced to merely the learning of linguistic competence for everyday occasions. The point of the critics was not that mundane competence was unimportant, but that it was not the same as literary appreciation, and indeed that competence arises in the natural course of more challenging literary studies.

These concerns over content were more specific to English than the dissatisfactions over assessment, although they obviously have features in common with the points made by teachers of computing. The Development Unit's response to these points was essentially to deny their relevance, by invoking an alleged view 'in the further education sector' that English was 'an academic, "literary" subject with its own special content, unrelated to "real world" communication needs'. They then claimed to have compared the skills actually developed in good English courses and good communications courses in further education, and concluded that they could all be fitted into the same broad framework.

None of the responses satisfied the teachers. At one meeting in Edinburgh in October 1997, matters became particularly acrimonious. The teachers present subjected the representative of the Development Unit to robust questioning, and she described this as 'unprofessional' and 'rude'. This provoked outrage among the teachers, and subsequent signed statements found none of them accepting the Development Unit's version of events: they agreed unanimously that the line of questioning had been perfectly legitimate. By the following autumn a petition originating from the group of teachers in Lothian, calling for the ending of the proposed internal assessments, had been signed by over 1,300 English teachers, nearly half of all English teachers in Scotland.

There is a real sense, looking at these exchanges, that the two sides were talking past each other. The teachers were motivated by the memory of the central role which their subject had played in Scottish education. This was a cultural role in which the development of the capacity to communicate in an instrumental way was a relatively minor outcome. What mattered was the preservation and handing on of a heritage, and the preparation of a new generation for the very broad-ranging tasks of renovating it. What motivated the Development Unit was the vocational purpose of equipping students with the linguistic skills that would enable them to be effective workers, something for which the study of literature was only one possible preparation, and – for most students – not necessarily a central one.

The Development Unit was missing the point with English. It

simply failed to acknowledge that the objections were offered as part of a reasoned educational critique of the proposals. The central arguments of the critics were never engaged with. The Development Unit continued to treat the dispute as being about technicalities. The objections to the internal assessments were responded to in a managerial sense (that these were no greater a burden than existing practice), not by seriously attempting to counter the educational arguments. There was no hint of an appreciation of the history and cultural purposes of an English curriculum. As a result of having their case effectively ignored in this way, English teachers felt increasingly frustrated and professionally insulted, and so the arguments were no longer really about details of assessment or the curriculum, but were more in fact about the status and role of teachers in educational reform. By leaving matters to the technical forums of the Development Unit, the inspectorate and ultimately the government were implicitly saying that the purposes of the entire reform were not officially open for debate. The aims and philosophy of Higher Still having been settled by the inspectors and the politicians, any objections which teachers raised could be about no more than the details of implementation.

The problems with mathematics were not so evident during the development phase of Higher Still, but became very controversial when the first new Higher exam paper was sat in May 2000. As with English, the root of the problem lay with an apparent mismatch between the internal assessments and what students were expected to do in the external exam. It was felt by mathematics teachers that students had not been prepared by the internal tests for the kind of exam that they faced. The internal assessments were set at a low level, which most students could pass fairly easily. The exam was quite different. Over the last decade or so, it has become accepted as good practice in assessing maths to provide an introductory part to each exam question where students can work their way into the problem and pick up a few marks. They are then prepared for the substantial and most difficult core. This approach has been shown to allow all students to demonstrate their full potential, while also stretching the brightest in the hard part at the end. It is the only approach consistent with providing 'opportunity for all'. Instead, what was issued in May 2000 was what one principal teacher (in correspondence with me) described as 'looking like a Higher paper from 20 years ago'. He went on: 'The examination was obviously written in haste and was very badly conceived,' and he described some questions as 'sadistic'. Another principal teacher pointed out that 'anyone can write an exam paper that has students in tears'. That many were in fact reduced to this state was evident in the press and on television during the days after the exam was sat.

These concerns about the exam in mathematics show that even the assessment philosophy of Higher Still had not always been thought through adequately, and was not always in touch with the most advanced thinking internationally, despite the claims of the Development Unit. That the outcome was seriously embarrassing was then acknowledged privately by the Scottish Executive Education Department in August 2000. It slipped out as part of its submission to the parliamentary inquiry into the crisis that a report on the difficulty of the maths paper was meant to have been issued along with the results on 10 August. But, in a letter to the chief executive of the SQA from Eleanor Emberson, the senior civil servant in the curriculum section of the department, it was agreed 'to look separately at arrangements for publicising the maths Higher report': 'I understand your reluctance to raise further press interest in the maths Higher by releasing the report just now.'

In November, well into the new school session, the verdict on mathematics 2000 was still awaited.

WORKLOAD

The most politically potent objection, and the one that came to be the focus of all the rest, was on the workload that the new courses would entail. This almost caused the entire reform to collapse, and may yet do so if the crisis of the year 2000 cannot be satisfactorily resolved.

The 1994 proposals on Higher Still were launched into an inauspicious environment in this respect, as we have seen from the immediate reactions by the two main unions. By the summer of 1994 the EIS had taken a decision to boycott all new developments in education, and so there was no official EIS involvement in the various implementation committees for several years. As teachers became increasingly dissatisfied with the educational content of what was being proposed, they were also being asked to work in a context where budgets were being squeezed very tightly. One background reason for that was the reform of local government which took place in 1996, abolishing the nine large regions that had governed education since 1975, and replacing them with 29 smaller authorities. (The three small island authorities remained largely untouched.) This reform was accompanied by cuts in local-authority finance over several sub-sequent years. For example, in March 1997 education budgets suffered a cut of 4 per cent in Aberdeen, 3 per cent in Edinburgh, 4 per cent in Glasgow, 7 per cent in Perth and Kinross and 3 per cent in Highland. Examples of what this meant in practice were the severe curtailment of visiting specialist teachers for primary and small rural secondaries (for example in music, art, drama and Gaelic), non-filling of mainstream teaching posts as they became vacant, and cuts in the maintenance of school buildings. These would have been difficult enough to absorb at the best of times, but were particularly awkward in the midst of such a massive new development. One effect of this, and of the loss of the economies of scale in the large regions, was the swift erosion of the previous educational advisory service. That was staffed by former teachers who would help their colleagues in schools by providing, for example, curricular materials or advice on teaching methods. The advisers had been regarded as crucial to the successful implemen-tation of Standard Grade. Their absence in the Higher Still development was acutely felt.

Until 1998 the only new money available to Higher Still was for national work – such as in the Development Unit and associated activities. It was not until September 1998 that a substantial sum was invested in school development, most of it going directly to schools to free teachers from some of their teaching in order to prepare for the new courses that were to start in summer 1999.

But it was immediately pointed out by union leaders that the money made available would be sufficient to free each teacher for only about one day in the whole year. Even with this £18 million for schools, it remained the case that far more − £26 million − had been invested in national developments.

The odd thing was that the growing anger of teachers during 1998 had not been foreseen. Looking through the press cuttings for the first half of 1998, it is difficult to find much reporting of Higher Still at all, in contrast to the voluminous material in the previous three years, especially around the time at which the detailed arrangements for particular subjects were set out and debated in the winter of 1995–96, and then again following the further postponement and extra investment in the national programme. This lack of attention may be because the activity during the session 1997–98 was mainly in the various training sessions which the Development Unit and the inspectorate were putting on for principal teachers (who were then expected to train the members of their own departments). On the one hand, this was of necessity not visible to outsiders, except in the unusual circumstances of the controversy over English and one or two other areas. On the other hand, this was precisely when most teachers came face to face with the actual demands of the new courses, three to four years after Ian Lang had issued the original policy statement. They were shocked at the workload implications. That was the price which Higher Still had to pay for denying that there would be any. Teachers could not but be taken aback after they had been told repeatedly that there was no need for most of them to be involved in development work.

Whatever the reason, the issue exploded onto the national stage again in June 1998 when the EIS conference voted to hold a ballot of its membership on a complete boycott of Higher Still. The other main union, the SSTA, soon followed suit. The ballots were scheduled for November. It was during the campaigning for the ballot that the minister announced some extra money, and she also agreed that some subjects (notably English) and some levels could be phased in (rather than starting in summer 1999). In effect, this was a third postponement: the official target was now that the programme would be in place by 2004, which would represent a seven-year delay from Ian Lang's original target. But the teachers were unimpressed. On a 61 per cent turnout, 86 per cent of the EIS voted for a boycott; the support in the SSTA was 78 per cent on a 59 per cent turnout. The reason why the last-minute funding and postponement seemed to have no effect is that, like the Development Unit, they missed the point. It was not really the workload issue as such that drove teachers to vote in such overwhelming majorities for such a drastic step. That ballot became a focus of all the more directly educational issues, and of the sense that they had not been adequately consulted over any serious aspect of the reform. They felt devalued.

They probably felt even more devalued by what happened next. The EIS started its boycott on 1 December. Three days later, it and the other unions accepted an invitation to join a new Higher Still Liaison Group, chaired by Douglas Osler, the head of the inspectorate, and also including representatives of the head-teachers, local authorities, colleges, parents and the Scottish Office. The boycott was suspended on the same day. The SSTA lifted its a fortnight later. That 'suspension' is still the official position. This tension between membership and union leadership was inevitable in the circumstances, but the circumstances are precisely what have to be questioned. The union leadership believed that a sustained boycott at that stage would have destroyed the Higher Still policy altogether, and would also have endangered the union's influence in the parallel talks on teachers' pay and conditions. The point at which to have reconciled this position with its members' frustration would not have been in December 1998. It would have been much earlier, by involving teachers in the development of Higher Still from the start. That this would have been very difficult – because of the EIS's previous boycott of new developments – should have indicated the sheer difficulty of introducing this reform so quickly after so much turmoil in Scottish education over the previous two decades. But the anger of the membership, and the real dilemmas of the leadership, were not of their own making. They were ultimately a consequence of teachers' not being at the heart of Scottish educational policy.

The phasing turned out to be a clever move politically, because it divided the opposition, allowing the less contentious exams to be brought in immediately, and thus allowing the reform to commence. The first courses started in August 1999, so the first awards were due a year later.

That teachers had been motivated primarily by educational issues during the previous five years of debate was shown by their application in the ensuing months: no one has questioned their dedication in making the new courses work, even though things started to go wrong immediately in the administration from the SQA. Teaching materials arrived late, especially examples of what would count as a successful performance in either the internal assessments (those parts of the course that were tested by the teachers themselves) or the external exam that was to take place in late spring 2000.

In fact, neither the external nor the internal assessment arrangements were working out as planned. A system of external assessment can work effectively only if teachers know at the beginning of the course exactly what criteria will be used to judge candidates: in many subjects, this information was not available until well into the session. There was not enough information to allow teachers to conduct their own informal tests – so-called 'formative' assessment, which is used to find out where each student's strengths and weaknesses are, so as to allow the teacher to indicate to them where they need to make more progress. In previous years all these materials had arrived in time for the beginning of the school session.

But if there were problems with providing information that would allow teachers to prepare their students for the external examinations, the situation concerning the formal internal assessments – or 'unit assessments' as they were officially called – was approaching the chaotic. Students had to pass all the unit assessments in a course before they were allowed to sit the external exam in May 2000. Yet the arrangements for these crucial tests were awry from the start. Some of the assessment instructions were actually changed after the assessments were due to have taken place. Students found themselves being assessed almost all the time: a typical student taking around five subjects, each with an average of half a dozen internal assessments, would have faced on average about one assessment every school week from late October to April. Not surprisingly, schools then found themselves under pressure from parents to delay individual assessments until the students were ready. That may seem unacceptable educationally, but parents were doing no more than insisting on an extension into fifth and sixth year of the rules about assessment that have now been officially established in primary and early secondary, where pupils are formally tested only when the teacher judges them to have reached a level that would allow them to pass the test. The frequency of internal assessments was compounded for students who failed the test first time round. There was little time for them to recover, resit the test, and then – if they were successful – move onto the next test. As North Lanarkshire council officially complained to the Higher Still Liaison Group in February 2000, 'unit assessments mean that, in many cases, students see the part but not the whole'.

Crucially, the system of 'moderation' seems simply to have collapsed. Moderation is supposed to be the way in which the marking standards of individual teachers are checked against a national standard; it is a vital part of any system of internal assessment (for example, it is the normal practice in universities). It was supposed to have been integral to Higher Still. And yet, in the words of the official submission to the parliamentary inquiry by South Lanarkshire council, 'The moderation process was almost wholly discredited. Little moderation was carried out, and moderation results were often not intimated [to schools] until much later, even after the course exam date.'

No official acknowledgement of these problems was ever forthcoming during the session. But as early as November 1999 the head of the Higher Still Development Unit, Mary Pirie, circulated a lengthy letter to headteachers that was clearly a response to the concerns which schools had been expressing. The tone was not encouraging. On what to do about students who were failing the first unit assessments, it had this to say: 'The timing of initial assessment has been too early in some cases for students to have attained a new and challenging level.' In other words, the fault lay with the teacher for putting the students forward too soon, not with the design of the assessments.

On the lack of formative assessment, the letter commented that the official test items from the National Assessment Bank held by the SQA 'were not intended for diagnostic use', and 'for the longer term, lessons will hopefully have been learned about the timing, particularly of first assessments', which may have been fine for the future, but was not much help for students who were already in the courses.

On the rapidity of assessments, Ms Pirie's letter had this advice to teachers for students who had failed the first in the series: 'The best strategy is to delay reassessment of Unit 1 till there is confidence that the student is ready, for example by rolling it up with assessment of Unit 2.' This image of assessment as a sort of layered pancake has no known educational basis. The obvious question arises: if they could be 'rolled up' like this, why were they separate in the first place?

Pressure from parents was also blamed on teachers: 'Pressure on reassessment deadlines is reported to be compounded where schools have raised parents' expectations about detailed progress reports and completion dates.'

On the 'wider issue of staff confidence', the advice was to use staff meetings to air 'insecurities', and to rely on advice from the external moderators who were meant to check teachers' marking standards (and who, it now transpires, were a rare species). In fact, we now know from evidence submitted to the parliamentary inquiry that teacher 'insecurities' were not really taken seriously at all. When the EIS reported to a meeting of the Liaison Group in September 1999 that the EIS conference in June had voted to end all internal assessments, the Group did no more than 'note' what was said. At a meeting in February 2000 of one of the committees that were spawned by the Liaison Group, the School Assessment Focus Group, the official comment on the anxieties that were expressed by the teacher unions was that these were 'an understandable, and probably temporary, loss of confidence. It was felt that this might simply be a normal and transitory consequence of any change process.'

Yet again, the blame was seen to lie with the teachers, and the solution to be in counselling rather than in altering the system.

But if the unit assessments were causing educational problems, rumbling in the background was what happened to the data that emerged from them. This, of course, is what eventually erupted in disaster in August 2000. The EIS, in its submission to the parliamentary inquiry, is quite clear that there was early evidence that things were going drastically wrong. The simple act of registering candidates in the autumn of 1999 was confused, data being sent by schools and then lost by the SQA. The problems started to mount in January and February 2000, when schools tried to update their lists of candidates and the SQA repeatedly failed to record the changes. For example, it kept on including the names of students who had left school six months previously. But then the real mess started to grow. In the words of the EIS submission: 'Teachers were asked for and supplied the results of specific units, on up to four different occasions, sometimes by fax, email, post and telephone. The SQA seemed repeatedly incapable of processing basic data. The problem was clearly not resolved by the end of the school session at the end of June.'

The EIS notes that, in August, it was immediately obvious to many teachers that the basic problem with the results was that whole swathes of data on internal assessments had simply not been entered into the SQA computer. Without evidence that a student had passed all the internal elements, the computer would automatically assume that he or she had failed.

This EIS evidence is corroborated by the submissions from the local authorities. Angus Council, for example, notes that headteachers had been expressing concerns about data management at the SQA early in the 1999–2000 session. Argyll and Bute said that all its secondary schools had experienced problems with SQA data management. Highland Council pointed out that school data was repeatedly not picked up by the SQA. South Lanarkshire said that some of its schools had been asked to resubmit data no fewer than seven times, and one school had had 60 separate contacts with the SQA to clarify and verify information on a particular course. West Lothian had experienced problems with information transfer to the SQA as early as October 1999, and had placed that issue as a standing item on the agenda of the monthly meetings of the local Higher Still Steering Group. And, as the EIS put it with eloquent understatement, 'Long before the whole issue became public, the events were a cause of concern for many teachers.' Moray Council concluded that the SQA training events and presentations to schools had been no better than a public relations exercise.

Even more damning is the evidence that we now have that the SQA, the Education Department and senior schools inspectors were aware of the data-management problems right from the start of the session. At a meeting of the Liaison Group in September 1999 the representative of one of the small unions, Maureen Laing of the Professional Association of Teachers, reported that some of the unit assessments were available on the Internet (thus compromising the integrity of the whole process); the entire response from Ron Tuck, chief executive of the SQA, was that 'it was regrettable if this happened'. On 23 November 1999 a meeting took place between Carolyn Hutchinson, an inspector, and Neil MacGowan, a senior manager at the SQA, about concerns that had been raised with the Scottish government about the SQA's systems for receiving and processing data from schools. This meeting took place with the approval of the head of the inspectorate, Douglas Osler, and the assurance received from Mr MacGowan was reported back to him and to the Higher Still Liaison Group. But the inspectorate believed in February 2000 (in a report to the Liaison Group) that everything was going well, and that there were no major concerns.

Nevertheless, concerns continued to be expressed. The *Daily Mail* reported on 9 March 2000 that schools were experiencing serious problems with transferring data to the SQA, as did *The Herald* on 4 April. The official response from David Elliot, another senior manager at the SQA, was that 'we are confident that the exams will run properly, right through to the issuing of certificates'. Ron Tuck wrote to headteachers on 30 March grudgingly acknowledging the concerns, but not in fact admitting that any of them were serious, or that any would jeopardise the system: 'We know that in some cases schools have encountered software problems which have led to concerns over the accuracy of the candidate entry records held by the SQA. To allow centres to identify any errors or omissions we are producing paper reports of our current entry records and asking schools to check these against their own data files.'

But the public air of confidence was at odds with what Mr Tuck was being told by his own staff. On 3 March – four weeks before that letter to headteachers – one of the directors of the SQA had e-mailed Mr Tuck expressing grave misgivings about the entire data-management capability of the organisation: 'I'm reluctant to press the panic button, but I am becoming very worried.' And, privately, these concerns were shared by the Education Department. Alastair Wallace, secretary to the Liaison Group, and a civil servant in the Department, wrote to David Elliot on 20 April: 'We have been told recently that registration problems have affected teachers' confidence in the Higher Still programme as a whole.' There were also concerns about errors in the recording of results. In his letter, Mr Wallace referred separately to the press stories (in the *Daily Mail* and *The Herald*), and so it is clear that this information on teachers' confidence must have come to the Department from the inspectorate.

The SQA began to appreciate the scale of the problems by May. They cancelled a PR event called to celebrate the award of some certificates to candidates on short vocational courses because of media interest in the problems of their computing systems. And yet, as late as 1 June 2000, while students were finally sitting the first batch of external exams under the new system, David Elliot could announce to the Finance and General Purposes Committee of the SQA that 'progress to date [on data management] was satisfactory. Contingency plans had been prepared for every eventuality.'

We now know they hadn't. More to the point, so did the Education Department and the inspectorate. A meeting took place on 14 July with senior managers of the SQA, after which a letter was sent on 17 July to Ron Tuck from Eleanor Emberson of the Department. It purports to be a summary of the meeting, but has the tone of a series of instructions. (If it hadn't been that, it would presumably have been written by someone at the SQA.) It notes that, despite Mr Elliot's public confidence on 1 June, the results processing service was still causing him and his colleagues 'concern'. It is acknowledged that the checking of certificates needed to be supplemented in some way, and that, as a last resort, the scheduled date for issuing certificates (10 August) might have to be delayed. But Ms Emberson clearly had no faith in the problems being sorted out in time, because she added that 'we do not want the next problem to be an appeals backlog', and so insisted that the information issued by the SQA with the results should point out that it was possible to appeal against external assessments even if there were mistakes in the recording of unit results. She also added that 'perhaps the press ad on delays should avoid the phrase "sorry for any inconvenience"'. Whatever may be said about the Education Department, it clearly had a much more acute sense than the SQA of the public relations disaster that was looming.

But, as Ms Emberson expected, the problems were not cleared up. By 1 August the situation was still sufficiently uncertain that Alastair Wallace could write to Neil MacGowan that 'I do not know if the issue of the exam results will take place on 9 August as planned' and 'there is also the more general problem of how to manage public relations to avoid SQA and others being swamped by queries' about a delay, or 'for the more likely scenario that the results are issued on time but still with substantial numbers of incomplete certificates'. Even Mr Wallace assumed that there would be no inaccurate certificates, since he believed that evidence of inaccuracies would be found by the SQA and would lead to a delay in issuing results.

So the first year of Higher Still began to confirm some of the worst fears of teachers concerning the stress caused by the massive amount of internal assessment. It quickly became clear that the SQA's administration was not working efficiently, either to deliver important material that would allow teachers to assess their students correctly, or to receive the results of these tests back from schools. Schools raised these problems repeatedly, with their local authority, through the media, and through their regular contacts with the schools inspectorate based in the Scottish Executive Education Department. It is also clear that the inspectorate appreciated early on in the session (at least as early as November 1999) that the data-management problems were potentially very serious indeed. But the SQA repeatedly reassured everyone that everything would be fine. Teachers never believed this during the session: that is why the teacher representatives kept raising the matter at the Higher Still Liaison Group and similar forums. Neither did the local authorities. And, it appears from the activity which the inspectorate was undertaking, neither did it. But it was all too late. The fateful decision was to go ahead with the new courses in session 1999–2000, and that was taken – as we saw – in consequence of the phased introduction that Helen Liddell sanctioned in November 1998. That, in turn, was a reaction to the teachers' vote to boycott the whole reform. It is likely now that thousands of students, parents and teachers themselves now wish that that threatened boycott had been turned into a reality.

CONCLUSIONS

The first point to make about what then happened in August 2000 is that it was no more than the latest problem affecting Higher Still. To claim, as Douglas Osler, the head of the inspectorate, did before the parliamentary inquiry on 9 October, that 'Higher Still was successful up to the point at which young people completed their examination scripts', is to ignore the mass of detailed criticism which had been accumulating over six years. In a policy sense, the debacle in August 2000 was not even the most serious, although in terms of its human implications it was awesome.

There do not seem to have been any widespread advance warnings that precisely this kind of disaster would take place, presumably because the last thing which the SQA was believed to be unable to do was to run a results service. The first evidence that they might not have been able to do so does not seem to have come until autumn 1999, by which time it was too late: the courses were running, students were taking their internal assessments, and they were rushing towards the external exams in June with absolute inevitability.

But to separate the results-issuing crisis from the deeper criticisms of Higher Still that had been emerging for six years is not really plausible. The SQA's data-management systems were overwhelmed because of the scale of the internal assessments, something which had been criticised on educational grounds for at least five years. The lack of correspondence between the results of internal assessments and external examinations had also been part of the case against Higher Still that teachers and others had been making for some time. The ways in which the schools were overwhelmed by the management demands of the new system was what the unions and the local authorities had been warning about for years. It does not mitigate the force of that criticism to point out that the schools actually did not succumb to pressure, despite these warnings, and that they were even able to cope with more pressure when they had to administer the large number of extra appeals in September 2000. That it was the SQA, not the schools, where catastrophe actually occurred does add a touch of irony, in the light of the aura of competence and authority that those in charge of public policy like to convey. But the failure of teachers to forecast that the SQA would collapse under the strain does not detract from the larger validity of their prediction that *something* would. These warnings by teachers about overload are the main grounds for saying that what happened in summer 2000 was not inevitable.

It is also clear, looking back over the six years, that far more fundamental issues have been raised by Higher Still than just the management demands of a new assessment system, and that some of these deeper issues have not yet even begun to be tested in practice. For example, whether small schools will be able to offer all levels in all courses will not be obvious for several years, and the best that can be said at the moment is that the chaos in 2000 does not improve their chances of doing so. It may be fortuitous that the results crisis has caused all sorts of other deficiencies in the policy to be brought to the fore again. But that's politics, and is quite fair. The SQA is responsible for technical things, and failed. That puts all the things for which other people and institutions are responsible on the table again too. The teachers are responsible for the educational aspects, and yet felt that they were not being given a voice in precisely this area of their expertise. The inspectorate is responsible for developing the policy, and so has responsibility for its failures as well as for success. Students underwent enormous stress, as teachers had been predicting for a long time, and survived, which is more than can be said for the SQA's computers.

The most disturbing of these more fundamental conclusions to draw from the history of the reform between 1994 and 2000 is that there was never a tested consensus around its philosophy, mainly because the philosophy was never debated. Asking new questions about fundamental issues was not attractive to the Scottish consensus that had accepted Howie's analysis that the system needed revolutionising, and that mere incremental changes to the status quo were not enough. We return to this point in the next chapter, where we look at the political context in which Higher Still was being developed. The main point to take from this one is that there were many severe criticisms of Higher Still, voiced mainly by teachers. These remain valid, or at least remain reasons why a reform as fundamental as this ought to have been taken forward much more cautiously. In some respects, they point to doubts about the reform itself, since Howie's critique of modularisation has probably become much more widely accepted than it would have been in 1992. Turning everything into modules really does risk transforming education into an assessment-driven and stress-dominated mess. Whether we can now escape from it will be the subject of Chapter 7.

CHAPTER 5

The Political Context

Whatever went wrong in 2000 would have happened whether or not there had been a Scottish parliament in place. Direct political involvement in the policy of Higher Still had always been intermittent – a few postponements, some extra money now and again, but no real political leadership. It was not a matter that divided the parties, even at the 1997 general election when the big questions were the future of the Tory government and the prospect, if they fell, of a referendum on setting up a parliament. In the first election to the parliament, held in May 1999, the only educational issue that truly distinguished the parties from each other was over the charging of fees to students in higher education. Higher Still, with its alluring subtitle promising opportunity for all, was not at stake.

Even less at issue was the body which oversaw the 2000 crisis, the Scottish Qualifications Authority. As we have seen in the previous chapter, it was formed in 1997 by the merger of the two predecessor organisations which conducted exams in schools and further education colleges – the Scottish Examination Board and the Scottish Vocational Education Council. New legislation was needed for the merger, but was not contentious in a party-political sense. So uncontroversial was the new SQA's operation that it did not even rate a mention in an important critique of Scottish quangos issued in 1996 by the left-of-centre John Wheatley Centre (a report to which we return below). The SQA had attracted none of the controversy which had, under the Tories, dogged health boards, local enterprise companies or the water authorities.

But the mere existence of the Scottish parliament is bound to cause the current crisis to have far more extensive ramifications than it would have had under the old Scottish Office. Two of the parliament's committees held inquiries, whose reports will be influential over many years. These inquiries held all of their hearings in public, unlike the internal inquiries commissioned by the SQA itself and the Scottish government. The chamber of the full parliament has provided a forum in which some of the main points have been contested, perhaps most notably when Alex Salmond, then leader of the SNP, challenged the late Donald Dewar, the First Minister, to reconcile the claims that ministers had no responsibility for the SQA with a clause in the founding Act which appeared to give them the right to intervene directly. Whatever the correct interpretation (a point to which we will return), that clash made for effective political theatre, dramatising the abstruse legal point in a much more visible way than an article in a newspaper or a written question at Westminster. Asking an oral question of the Secretary of State at Westminster in the old days would have had to wait for several weeks (and indeed, on this occasion, for several months, because Westminster did not reconvene until nearly three months after the crisis blew up). Some of all these separate activities could have happened if Scotland had still been governed by the Scottish Office, but not all at the same time. The parliament made it all more vivid and immediate.

None of this was an accident, an opportunistic ploy on the part of opposition politicians. Some of the core arguments for setting up a parliament have been precisely to do with democratising the way in which policy is made, with challenging the alleged complacency of the civic élites which have governed Scotland in the unreformed Union, and, for education, with casting democratic light on the role of the inspectorate in policy-making. It was an accident that it was the SQA which provided one of the first real tests of the parliament's capacity to inquire into the workings of a key civic institution, but that it would do so eventually was inevitable. Indeed, it had already started to do that for the Scottish Arts Council in the autumn of 1999, over a controversy surrounding the funding of Scottish Opera. The parliamentary committee responsible for that investigation was, as it happened, the same as was responsible for the main inquiry into the SQA, and so it had cut its teeth. But, however important opera may be, the £10 million annual budget of Scottish Opera pales into relative insignificance when compared to the approximately £900 million spent on Scottish public-sector secondary schools, or even the £27 million annual budget of the SQA itself.

THE SCOTTISH PARLIAMENT AND CIVIC ACCOUNTABILITY

There have been many strands to the debate about a Scottish parliament – nationalism, the expression of a sense of Scottish community, and the growing anger during the 1980s and 1990s at Scottish left-of-centre voting preferences being overridden by a Conservative government which, after the mid-1980s, was never able to command more than about a quarter of the vote in Scotland. But the most relevant strand in this context is the democratising one, the claim that a Scottish parliament was needed to hold public bodies to account.

In one sense this argument was attractive to supporters of a parliament regardless of their other views. It could be advocated by nationalists as a way of making Scottish government more truly national, in the sense of truly popular. It could even appeal to a few Scottish Conservatives. In 1978, for example, two members of the Conservative shadow cabinet (Francis Pym and Leon Brittain) argued that a Scottish assembly might be justifiable on the grounds that 'the lines of responsibility must be absolutely clear so that the citizen is certain where power, authority and responsibility for any decision lie and from whom he should seek redress for any grievance'.

But this democratising argument has always appealed most of all to Labour advocates of a parliament, such leading politicians as John P. Mackintosh, Labour MP in the 1960s and 1970s; John Smith, former British Labour leader; Gordon Brown, Chancellor of the Exchequer in the Blair government; and – most consistently and eminently – Donald Dewar. Mr Dewar had this to say in an interview in *New Statesman* shortly before the referendum in 1997: 'I believe this [parliament] will strengthen the Union. But I don't argue it on those terms. I argue it in terms of greater democracy.'

Earlier, in 1988, in the speech which committed Labour to joining the Constitutional Convention that eventually led to the scheme that the 1997 referendum endorsed, Mr Dewar expressed the classical democratising argument succinctly: 'Administrative devolution has grown over the years, but there is a great need for parallel democratic control.'

Another eloquent statement of it was made by the journalist Peter Jones, Scottish correspondent of *The Economist*, writing in 1997 before the general election of that year: 'The new politicians [in the Scottish parliament] will have to contend with another part of Scotland's hidden sub-strata that devolution will expose to daylight. This is the Scottish establishment élite which has quietly got on with running the country while the politicians have ranted and raved.'

Such arguments were appealing to social democrats such as Mr Dewar because they provided a clear distinction from the nationalists. To say that is not to impugn his sincerity in disowning the motive of 'dishing the Nationalists' (again from his 1997 interview). It is simply to note that there needed to be non-nationalist arguments available to the likes of Donald Dewar, John Smith and Gordon Brown if the Labour movement was ever to be converted enthusiastically to supporting home rule, as they had been by 1997. Of course, it became easier to make the case during the Thatcher and Major years, because the rather abstract democratic case was made urgent by the contrast in political majorities in Scotland and England, and it also became easy at that time to obscure the essential difference between the democratic case and the nationalist one. But Mr Dewar and his colleagues needed the democratic argument to sustain the campaign for a parliament after Labour had come to power in 1997. Otherwise, they would have been open to the accusation that there was no longer any need for a parliament now that the Tories had gone.

There was no shortage of specifically educational examples to fuel this argument. Professor Walter Humes, in his book on the leadership class in Scottish education, illustrates it with the issue of the closing of Hamilton College of Education in the early 1980s. He quotes from the official record of the inquiry by the West-

minster Select Committee on Scottish Affairs to show the perma-
nent secretary of the Scottish Education Department, Angus
Mitchell, resolutely refusing to answer a Labour MP's questions
about the role of the minister, the Tory Alex Fletcher. The MP,
John Maxton, asked 'Are you telling me that the minister had no
involvement whatsoever in this?' to which the reply was: 'Not at
all. I am sorry but I cannot answer detailed questions as to the
involvement of ministers at any particular stage.' That was not a
sign of transparent government.

The hope of the campaigners for home rule was that the committees of a Scottish parliament would have the time, and would
develop the expertise, to extract much more forthcoming accounts
of how decisions were taken. These aspirations were embodied in
the standing orders and working practices which were put in
place for the parliament by the cross-party Consultative Steering
Group that reported in December 1998, based on the principle
that: 'The Scottish parliament should be accessible, open and
responsive, and develop procedures which make possible a
participative approach to the development, consideration and
scrutiny of policy and legislation.'

Doing this was felt to be desirable even by those – among
whom was Donald Dewar – who broadly admired the institutions
of civic Scotland. But the democratic argument was much stronger
among people who regarded civic Scotland as insufferably complacent. One of these is Professor Humes again. Although he
would probably not be counted as a passionate supporter of home
rule, he certainly was passionate in his identification of what was
wrong with Scottish educational politics in the unreformed
Union: 'Fear of what critical analysis might bring to the surface is
a feature of the Scottish national consciousness, unable to come to
terms with the many conflicting political and cultural pressures to
which it is subject.' The supporters of a parliament would then
argue that, by deliberately bringing these tensions into public,
Scottish politics and policy-making could be made much
healthier.

Such arguments have usually been combined with a scepticism
about the claimed strengths of Scottish education. It is alleged

that the civic élites are complacent, unwilling to listen to evidence that disturbs their assumptions of their own and the system's superiority, and deeply conservative behind a veneer of egalitarianism. So one of the purposes of setting up a Scottish parliament would be, according to this view, the puncturing of complacency, exposing the incompetence of the people who have run education in the Union, and forcing a proper public debate about how good the system really is and how it should be governed and managed.

The courses and examinations in fifth and sixth year at school could be cited as a test of this kind of argument. Howie's report dealt with the complacency, and the swift readiness to accept that analysis may have owed something to the same desire to renovate civic Scotland as produced the Scottish parliament seven years later. On the other hand, the policy as it developed was firmly in the hands of the same civic élites that had run Scottish education for a very long time. We will consider in a moment whether the apparent consensus that developed around Higher Still was in fact subjected to a thorough consultation, but for the time being the main point is that the people and institutions in charge of the reform were not radically different from the traditional governing class of Scottish education. The main difference now was that it all came apart to an unprecedented extent: the impression of effortless efficiency could never be given again. So the events of summer 2000 could be an ideal opportunity for the parliament to demonstrate that it was able to hold civic Scotland to account. Instead of having to search out complacency and lack of competence, it was presented with them ready-made.

QUANGOS
One important aspect to the democratising debate has been the role of quangos, an example of which is the Scottish Qualifications Authority. Defining a quango is notoriously difficult, since there are all sorts of public bodies that are on the margins of any definition: the usual full version of the acronym, 'quasi-autonomous, non-governmental organisation', does not really help. A useful working definition in this context was given by the

John Wheatley Centre committee of inquiry into the relationship between quangos and a Scottish parliament. It was chaired by Jean McFadden, who was then a lecturer in law at Strathclyde University and also a Labour councillor in Glasgow. The membership was fairly broadly representative of people in and around the Labour Party, including one local councillor who later became an MSP and Scottish Finance minister, Angus McKay. Another member was John McAllion, the radical Labour MSP. Writing in 1996, and so before the referendum, the committee defined the quangos that fell within their remit thus: 'a body, not elected by universal suffrage, which formally or de facto carries out executive functions in an area of public administration or policy which under the proposals of the Scottish Constitutional Convention would be allocated to the Scottish parliament, and whose members are currently appointed either directly or indirectly by the government'.

Generally there are two reasons why we have quangos in public life. The first is common throughout the UK, and grew up with the welfare state in the mid-twentieth century. The goal of social reformers was to find technical solutions to political problems. Politicians were regarded as a nuisance. With politicians in control, a community would get a hospital or a school because the local politicians could shout loudest, not because of any real need. The way to avoid this kind of special pleading was to appoint committees of experts. Medical scientists would decide where the need for health services was greatest. Professional educationalists would allocate grants to universities, or set examinations for schools. In carrying out these activities, the professionals would refer to universal criteria of need, or fairness, or objectivity – the kind of principles with which any reasonable and non-partisan person would agree. This liking for committees of experts and agreed rules now seems naively utopian. But it was a view that appealed right across the political spectrum.

In Scotland, moreover, quangos were regarded enthusiastically for a second reason. They could preserve Scottish distinctiveness. The professionals on the Scottish committees would adapt central-government policies to Scottish conditions. They could be trusted to do this by the government precisely because they were 'experts'. And they could be trusted by the Scots themselves because the Scottish professions remained distinctive, with their own special traditions and practices.

Given this broad, non-partisan history of support for the general principle of quangos, it is not surprising that the John Wheatley Centre inquiry concluded that they do have a role because they are independent from day-to-day government pressure, can provide specialist expertise that government would not normally possess, can take initiatives quickly, can take a broad view over several areas of government policy, and can act as a forum in which specialist public-interest groups can take part in debate with each other and with government. Their main disadvantage, according to the committee, was a lack of accountability, their susceptibility to political cronyism, their vulnerability to vested interests, and an excuse for 'ministers to shelter behind the quasi-autonomous status to prevent effective scrutiny by other elected representatives'. There was no such thing as genuinely undisputed expertise. One person's technical competence is somebody else's conspiracy.

In response to this, the committee recommended various detailed ways of improving the accountability of quangos. Among these were that there should be a Public Appointments Committee that could monitor the appointments to quangos. Quangos should be governed by the same principles of transparency as apply to local authorities, by which they meant that 'all committee meetings, papers and agendas should be open to the public', except where personnel matters and a few other genuinely confidential topics were concerned. Quangos should be subject to annual review by the relevant committee of the Scottish parliament. And public-interest groups of both a specialist and general type should be allowed to recommend, elect or appoint members of quango boards.

Nevertheless, the prospects of radical change of this sort would depend on political will, and some other writers have pointed to the various pressures that might prevent the Scottish parliament opening quangos up to full scrutiny. Richard Parry, an authority on social policy at Edinburgh University, argued in an article in the journal *Scottish Affairs* in 1999 that there was a great deal of inertia, if only because 'one theme of devolution is in part a response to innovation fatigue in public services'. He pointed out further that all politics – and especially New Labour politics – at the moment is more concerned with outputs than with processes, and so the pressure on quangos will have more to do with ensuring that they get certain things done than with *how* they do them. Parry nevertheless concludes that the parliament would slowly move to look at the 'gap between spending power and accountability', if only because inquiries by parliamentary committees would gradually open up quango business to public view.

The SQA could hardly be a better example of the forces of inertia: there was absolutely no pressure at all to hold it to detailed account before it spectacularly did not get things done in summer 2000. Its board is appointed by the government to represent the various interests in education, although no interest group has a right to nominate members or even to be present at all. One of the few criticisms that were made of the founding legislation was that it did not seem to guarantee educational experience on the board, unlike the regulations setting up the Examination Board, where places were specifically designated for teachers and other named groups. The chairman in 2000 was David Miller, not previously known for any notable educational expertise: he is also chairman of Wolverhampton & Dudley Breweries and a director of the insurance company Scottish Life. He had originally been appointed by the previous Conservative government to be chairman of both the Exam Board and the Vocational Education Council. When appointed to the former, he admitted that he was 'not an educationist', and the then chief executive of the Vocational Education Council said that his skills lay in 'putting people at ease'. No doubt these were in heavy demand in the summer of 2000. Nevertheless, several of the other board members did have significant and current educational experience – for example, four headteachers, a college principal and vice-principal, a university vice-principal, three other academics, the conveners of two local-government education committees, and the secretary of the STUC's education committee. This was fairly typical of the kinds of people who are appointed to quango boards generally.

The chief executive also had emerged from a solidly educational background. Ron Tuck started his career as a lecturer in the further education college in Angus, having taken a politics degree at Edinburgh University. He became an inspector in 1985, and was an adviser to the Howie committee. He was then the natural choice as the inspector who was put in charge of implementing Higher Still. He won the post of chief executive of the embryonic SQA in late 1996 in open competition against several internal candidates. David Miller described him as having a 'fantastically clear mind and good organisational ability'. Judith Gillespie, then a leader of the Scottish Parent Teacher Council, voiced the widespread view that he is also 'very amenable, restrained, jovial and with a willingness to absorb criticism'.

So, despite the upheaval represented by the merger of the Examination Board and Vocational Education Council, the SQA and its chief executive were not untypical of the members and senior staff of Scottish quangos, nor in a political sense a sharp departure from previous practice. They seem to have been appointed mostly for their expertise; apart possibly from the chairman, there was no evidence that, on this occasion, the Tories were disproportionately appointing their party supporters. And Mr Miller was not in any obvious way connected to the party: he was unusual only because all the previous chairmen of the Examination Board had been senior educationists.

The new body was like the Exam Board in one other important respect as well, which serves further to show how ambiguous is the independence of quangos. The legislation setting it up continued to give the government a strong power to direct its activities, a power that it had had in relation to the Exam Board since 1963 (as we saw in the Chapter 2). The relevant clause 9 says this: 'The Secretary of State may, after consultation with the SQA, give the SQA directions of a general or specific character with regard to the discharge of its functions and it shall be the duty of the SQA to comply with such directions.'

A further clause (7b) required the SQA to 'have regard to the interests of persons using its services'. (These powers passed to the Scottish government under the Scotland Act of 1998.)

The Scottish education minister steering the legislation through Westminster was Raymond Robertson, who commissioned legal advice from parliamentary counsel as to the extent of the powers which this wording conferred. Counsel's advice was unambiguous: the clause means exactly what it appears to mean. Mr Robertson then advised the relevant committee at Westminster that the duty to pay attention to the interests of users was wide-ranging, and that: 'it will be for the SQA itself to determine how to meet the duty in a particular case, though they would have to have regard to any advice which the Secretary of State might give on this question'.

This formal emphasis on directions is, however, potentially misleading, and allowed the Scottish government to claim in October 2000 that the powers thus given to ministers were for use only in dire emergencies – what one civil servant described as a 'nuclear option'. Ministers do not usually exercise any of their powers directly themselves, and in that sense almost all ministerial powers could be described as 'nuclear'. The main function of such clauses is to sanction the routine involvement not of the minister but of the minister's agents, namely here the civil servants and inspectors in the Education Department. When an inspector provides advice to a quango like the SQA, this is given with the authority of the minister, and in the terms of the founding legislation. That is why, as we saw in the previous chapter, inspectors were closely involved with the SQA over its data management from November 1999 onwards. Further back, it is why the inspectors were able to be so closely involved in the entire development of Higher Still. For example, the standard format of all the training sessions for principal teachers between 1998 and 1999 was a seminar led by the Higher Still Development Unit, with an inspector present to deal with policy issues and to report back to the Department.

So the SQA was both independent, exactly as the theory of quangos says it ought to be, and close to government. In developing the assessment for Higher Still, it was carrying out government policy. The government's interest in this was maintained routinely by the inspectors and other civil servants. But only on occasion would the minister be involved directly.

EDUCATION POLICY-MAKING

These discussions about democratising public life, and about quangos, raise some more general issues to do with the way in which educational policy is made, and which also have a bearing on how the Scottish parliament might change things. Policy-making is a lot more complex than the simple theory of liberal democracy would suggest. In theory, policy is made by governments, who are in turn elected by the people through the national parliament. In this view, civil servants (including specialists such as schools inspectors) are responsible only for carrying out the politicians' wishes.

But this theory is no more than a partial truth, an ideal to which our democracies only approximately conform. The main alternative theory is so-called 'pluralism'. According to this, policy is made by bargaining among government, civil servants and interest groups. Sometimes governments do not even initiate the discussions, and sometimes the bargaining leads to significant modifications to what the government originally wanted.

There are plenty of examples of this pluralism happening in Scottish educational policy. One that is particularly relevant in the present context is the way in which the original National Certificate modular courses were introduced from 1984. As was noted in Chapter 2, these were devised by the inspectorate. It was an initiative taken by the inpectors, and used by them to resist an encroachment on the powers of the Scottish Office from the Manpower Services Commission in Sheffield. The politicians went along with it probably for three main reasons. One was that the inspectorate took great care to assemble a consensus behind the move. The second was that the Conservatives, even then, were keen to put themselves on the side of any Scottish consensus which did not stand directly in the way of Thatcher's main ideological programme. And that was the third reason: the

National Certificate Scheme could be readily presented in Whitehall as a Scottish way of furthering Thatcherism, since it conceded the principle of a greater vocational relevance in school courses. That it then also defended the autonomy of Scottish education, and gave space for vocationalism to be introduced in a way that would not threaten comprehensive education and the developing Standard Grade, was a bonus that allowed the Conservatives to suggest that they were not as inimical to Scottish traditions as their opponents alleged.

The pluralism in all this lay in the bargaining which took place among government, inspectorate and interest groups. On this occasion, the inspectorate probably acted mainly as the voice of civic Scotland, presenting its view to Scottish Office ministers. (We don't know for certain, since the relevant government papers remain secret.) But, whatever the precise dynamics, there is no escaping the creativity of the inspectors. They devised the policy, pulled in the consensus and persuaded ministers. None of that was in any sense improper: at no point were they acting against government policy. But they led in the making of policy nonetheless.

The other main way in which the theory of policy-making is not a full description of what happens is in the important question of how policy is implemented. A policy is not just an Act of Parliament or a ministerial statement. It is also how it has an impact on real people. So how an educational policy is translated into practice is at least as important as what the policy statements say. This is where the role of the inspectorate is critical and inescapable. Its duties were most recently set out in a statement to parliament by the Secretary of State for Scotland in 1992, which was quoted in 1999 in an article by the recently retired head of the inspectorate, Nisbet Gallacher:

- evaluating and reporting publicly on the performance of individual educational institutions and of the system as a whole;
- identifying national developments needed in education, and providing leadership in carrying these developments out;
- providing professional policy advice to the minister.

The last of these relates to the policy-development role we have just been noting. The second relates to that too, but also indicates the scope for independent action. If a new policy, whether or not stemming from ministers, needs concomitant 'developments', it is quite clearly the responsibility of the inspectorate to provide these. It would then be the inspectors' job to evaluate whether the developments were being put in place, a task which would include checking the quality of the relevant work in schools. Mr Gallacher also pointed out that the policy advice which inspectors give to ministers includes the 'desirability and practicability in educational terms' of what the ministers intend to do. On Higher Still, specifically, he said that the inspectorate had taken 'a lead role in implementation'.

So, when the current head of the inspectorate, Douglas Osler, replied to a question during the parliamentary inquiry into the exams crisis that the inspectorate did not make policy, he was being disingenuous. The question came on 9 October from Mike Russell, an SNP member: 'Is this not a closed circle, Mr Osler? You have essentially said that you take in a range of comments, which you then sift. You take the sifted comments to the minister, who then asks you to do something that might include taking in a range of comments. That puts you back to where you started. In such a closed circle, it is possible that you are simply hearing what you want to hear – which is a phrase that several witnesses have used – and then passing that on to the minister, who then asks you to do what you want to do.'

Osler's reply was to deny that he and his colleagues made policy. Their job, he said, is not generating policy, but giving influential and important advice on policy. But, in an earlier reply to Mr Russell, he had also said: 'I want to return to the comment that [the inspectorate] was determined to force through Higher Still. [The inspectorate] has no reason at all to pick a programme such as Higher Still and decide that its role is to push it through. Successive education ministers asked the inspectorate to co-ordinate the implementation of Higher Still. That was carried out through the strategy group, the implementation group and eventually the liaison group, all of which included representatives from all the main stakeholders. We oversaw the implementation of Higher Still on behalf of ministers; [the inspectorate] has no vested interest in pursuing the programme.'

These exchanges sum up well the inspectorate's crucial and highly influential role in implementation. Mr Osler is quite clear that the inspectorate had a leading role in implementing Higher Still, and that its advice to ministers is usually very influential in shaping how ministers see the education system. That much was confirmed by one of the ministers for whom Mr Osler worked, Brian Wilson. In an interview with the *Times Educational Supplement Scotland* in August 1998, after he had left office, he said that: 'The general message I kept receiving was of general support for Higher Still. However, I do accept that I should have been more sceptical about the reassurances which were brought to me about the progress towards implementation.'

This weight of advice was all the more persuasive to the politicians because the inspectorate was the main element of continuity during the development of Higher Still. There were five education ministers, three Secretaries of State for Scotland, a change of UK government and the setting up of the Scottish parliament, altogether entailing massive political upheaval. But the inspectorate remained intact. Even the change of head from Mr Gallacher to Mr Osler does not alter that point, since Mr Osler was already a very senior and influential inspector before he was given the leading post.

In short, whether the influential role of the inspectors amounts to being a 'generator of policy' or a necessary adjunct to policy is beside the point: both activities are important, and both do a great deal to shape education. But the activities which Mr Osler admitted to before the parliamentary committee would probably be described by most people as simply policy-making.

POLICY-MAKING IN HIGHER STILL
All this brings us to the question about whether Higher Still was as widely accepted as is usually claimed (and as many of us believed until the summer of 2000). On the face of it, this initiative was an unusually democratic exercise in making policy,

anticipating by several years the attempt at a more transparent style of politics which the Scottish parliament is attempting to achieve. There truly was an unprecedented amount of consultation. But this has been described by David Raffe and Cathy Howieson of Edinburgh University, writing in the jorunal *Scottish Affairs* in 1998, as 'an exercise in democratic centralism'. The consultation was only over technical matters, not fundamental principles or philosophy. There was, for example, no consultation over the underlying philosophy of assessment – over whether it was educationally desirable to replace lengthy exams at the end of a course with a much shorter exam and lots of unit assessments. Some of the people whom Raffe and Howieson interviewed in their study of the policy felt that the consultations were used to justify decisions that had already been taken. Elsewhere, Raffe has called the consultation 'passive' – the invitation to comment on an agenda which had been drawn up elsewhere.

And when we ask where it had been drawn up, we are back at the inspectorate and the Higher Still Development Unit, which itself had been set up and was overseen by the inspectorate. Several of the submissions to the parliamentary inquiry would have agreed with Mike Russell's point in the question quoted above: that the inspectorate is charged by the minister to collect evidence, but then feeds the minister what it wants him or her to hear because it is responsible for collating and summarising the evidence. Judith Gillespie, the parents' leader and member of the Higher Still Liaison Group, has expressed astonishment at the rosy picture of progress on implementing Higher Still which the inspectorate was still presenting to the Group in February 2000. She would also argue that it chose to report what it wanted to see, a flagship policy sailing purposefully towards its destination, not a broken wreck about to sink with all hands. Constructing what we might call a social consensus is a lot more difficult than inviting comments on a predefined list of items, as the Consultative Steering Group on the Scottish parliament's procedures recognised, writing about legislation but in terms that would apply to any kind of policy: 'Once detailed legislative proposals have been published, it is extremely difficult for outside organisations to influence changes to those proposals to any great extent. What is desired is an earlier involvement of relevant bodies from the out- set – identifying issues which need to be addressed, contributing to the policy-making process and the preparation of legislation.'

THE IMMEDIATE POLITICAL CONTEXT
The way in which the parliament made a difference to how the evolving crisis was debated in August 2000 depended in part on the party-political balance there, and on the personalities. Labour led the Scottish government in coalition with the Liberal Demo- crats, a consequence of the proportional electoral system that was used for the elections in May 1999. Labour had dominated Scot- tish politics for the previous three decades, and had sympathisers throughout parts of Scottish life that would have been over- whelmingly Tory in England. Labour is the natural party of govern- ment in Scotland, led by such respectable and transparently honest politicians as John Smith, Donald Dewar, Gordon Brown and Robin Cook. But its electoral dominance was largely because its vote is efficiently concentrated, enabling it to win vast majorities of Scottish seats for Westminster, and seats in local councils, while attracting no more than a minority of the vote. For example, in the 1983 general election it had won 41 of the 72 par- liamentary seats (57 per cent) with only 35 per cent of the vote. By contrast, in the Scottish parliament election, it won 43 per cent of the seats with 36 per cent of the vote. The psychological effect of this loss of majority on some parts of the Labour Party was enormous, and the resulting necessity of having to negotiate a coalition with the much smaller Liberal Democrats was even more of an anathema to Labour members in west-central Scotland where that party barely exists.

The frustration arising from this dent to the image of Labour impregnability in Scotland was exacerbated by the aura of author- ity that New Labour under Tony Blair has been trying to cul- tivate. Since he took over the leadership in 1994, the entire effort of Labour's publicity machine has been to persuade voters that the party is competent enough to govern, and since 1997 the effort has gone into showing that it is truly in charge. So finding that it was not wholly in charge after May 1999 in Scotland (as in Wales) was a further blow to Labour's self-confidence.

That was then made even worse by the first year of the operation of the parliament. The Scottish government seemed to lurch from crisis to crisis. It seemed to choose the wrong issues on which to fight, and not to anticipate when a fight would be needed. For example, it announced a repeal of Tory legislation that had prevented local authorities from promoting homosexual relationships as an acceptable form of family without appreciating the controversy that this would cause for sex education in schools. The government seemed unable to control the squabbling of its own special advisers, two of whom were forced to resign. And it seemed not to be in control of the costs of the new building that will house the parliament at Holyrood.

Some of the accusations were, no doubt, unfair, and some segments of the media did tend to concentrate on essentially trivial matters at the expense of debating government policy proposals. For example, neither the government nor the parliament itself was responsible for the civil service decision to award medals to the new MSPs in summer 1999, and yet this was held up to ridicule by the press. But being able to survive criticism over small matters is precisely the mark of a secure régime. That the Labour-led government in Scotland did not feel secure was apparent to everyone. So the last thing it needed in the summer of 2000 was a genuine crisis of competence, and yet the failure to administer examination results correctly was exactly that.

For all these reasons, government ministers had to try to convey an impression of being in control. The inclination to do so was probably even greater because of the character of the particular minister who was then responsible for schools, Sam Galbraith. Asked by Douglas Fraser, political editor of the *Sunday Herald*, whether he took responsibility for the crisis, his reply was simple: 'Absolutely.' Mr Galbraith's style when he had been health minister in the old Scottish Office was to disarm critics by immediately acknowledging problems, in order then to put himself in charge of sorting them out. This is unconventional, but, as Mr Fraser observed, 'When you view the world as Galbraith does, the celebrities who present TV news are to be treated, like every-one else, as if they are nervous medical students facing the irritable bedside manner of the star neurosurgeon on his ward rounds.'

For the key point about Mr Galbraith is that, before he was elected to the Westminster parliament in 1987, he was a consul-tant neurosurgeon. That has shaped his entire approach to educa-tion and to politics. He castigates teachers for not keeping up to date with research in the way that doctors do, and he castigates educational researchers for sloppy work and results that have no relevance to the classroom. As Mr Fraser went on to note, 'It is that kind of disdain which sees Galbraith on holiday at the most important point in the school calendar, knowing that this year there is a particularly high risk of serious problems.' He was preparing to take on the teachers over pay and conditions: in return for higher salaries, he was pressing them to accept working conditions that would have involved a lot more compulsory train-ing courses. Teachers object, not because they are reluctant to keep their skills and knowledge up to date, but because they believe that, like doctors, each teacher should be in charge of what kind of professional development to engage in.

Thus, asserting authority was the Scottish government's tactic here, for political reasons and for reasons associated with the minister's own political style. The problem, of course, was that challenging Labour's authority was becoming one of the main roles of the Scottish parliament. If Labour had benefited dispro-portionately from the old electoral system, its main rivals, the SNP, had equally suffered. In the 1997 general election, the Nationalists had received only 6 seats (8 per cent) for 22 per cent of the vote. The SNP competes directly with Labour for left-of-centre, working-class votes, and so the feud between the parties is intense. In few places is it more bitter than in Govan, the seat which the SNP's education spokeswoman until early October, Nicola Sturgeon, had contested in the Scottish parliament elec-tions. She failed narrowly to win it from Labour, but was elected under the proportional part of the vote. For the SNP, Labour is the Scottish establishment, and denting its authority is precisely what it sees itself as having to do. Its position of being the main opposition in the Scottish parliament gave it a new platform in this task.

The problem for the SNP, however, has been that on social and economic policies it shares the same social democratic ground as Labour. Only on the constitution do the parties differ, most Labour members and MSPs being adamantly opposed to the SNP's policy of Scottish independence (although surveys show that around a third of Labour voters agree with the SNP on that). So, to win power in the Scottish parliament, the SNP's best chance is to show that Labour simply cannot deliver the social justice that both parties favour. One of the tactics is to show that key powers remain at Westminster – for example, over taxation and social security – and that New Labour there is insufferably cautious. But another tactic, now that Labour is in power in Scotland, is simply to show that its politicians are incompetent. So the exams crisis was a godsend. Here, on a matter affecting hundreds of thousands of young people and their families, was a potentially damning indictment of the inability of the old Scottish establishment in general, and Labour in particular, to run the country efficiently. Even better would be to pin explicit blame on the minister: if he could be shown to have known in advance about the impending disaster, then Labour's sincerity as well as competence would be brought into question.

The SNP was also looking for a way of distancing itself from that Scottish establishment. Any nationalist party in conditions other than those of an extreme dictatorship has a problem with the existing institutions of the nation. On the one hand, it cannot afford to denigrate them too severely, because that would seem to be rejecting some of the achievements of the nation on whose behalf it claims to speak. Thus the SNP frequently refers to the achievements of Scottish education. On the other hand, being too respectful of these institutions risks endorsing the very constitutional settlement which it opposes: if Scottish education is that good, it might be asked, what's wrong with the Union in which it flourished? One way out of this dilemma is to distinguish between the cautious élites who run the education system and the mass of teachers who make it work. The exams debacle presented precisely this opportunity. Teachers had been warning about disaster and had been ignored by the inspectorate and the Education Department. The inspectorate and the civil servants were now close to the Labour-led government. So the obvious line for the SNP to take was to present itself as the champion of the teachers and of the best traditions of Scottish education that were being betrayed by the current mess. This cultural angle appealed particularly to Mike Russell when he became education spokesperson for the SNP after John Swinney was elected leader.

The other key player in the political debates was Brian Monteith, education spokesman for the Scottish Conservatives. During the referendum in 1997 on setting up the parliament, he had in fact led the No campaign, but now was one of the 18 Tories who were elected in May 1999 (they were joined by one by-election victor in 2000). The Tories had – and still have – enormous difficulties, having come to be associated in Scotland with deeply unpopular policies during the long years in which they ruled at Westminster. For example, their legislation to allow schools to leave local-authority control was never attractive in Scotland and led to only two small schools doing so. And yet they could remember the not-too-distant days in the 1950s when they could command a majority of the Scottish popular vote. The new leadership in the Scottish parliament set about discreetly distancing itself from William Hague's English party, essentially by beginning to establish itself as the party of moderate Scottish patriotism. Mr Monteith was a key part of this strategy. He sounds Scottish (unlike some of the people who had dominated the Scottish Tories in the 1980s), he is an avid football supporter, and he sends his own children to public-sector schools. For him, the SQA crisis turned into an ideal opportunity to present his party as being on the side of Scottish education against the Labour establishment.

Mr Monteith also had other reasons to distrust the educational élites. He had been an adviser to Michael Forsyth when he was in the Scottish Office, and Forsyth was the only minister in that Office who had genuinely tried to open it up to greater public scrutiny in ways not involving a Scottish parliament. His solutions were not in the mainstream of the social-democratic and nationalist ethos of Scottish politics: he preferred markets to the ideas of accountability through a new parliament. Walter Humes, writing in the journal *Scottish Affairs* in 1995, has concluded of Forsyth's period as education minister in the late 1980s and early 1990s that he did indeed shake up educational policy to an unprecedented extent, but that he seriously underestimated the cultural resistance that his ideas would provoke. The old leadership class then regrouped following Forsyth's departure as the minister in 1992, and managed to take control again under his much more emollient successor James Douglas Hamilton. When Forsyth himself returned as Secretary of State in 1995, the political position of the party was just too precarious to resurrect his old campaigns, but the power of that élite resistance remained as a memory in Scottish Conservative ranks.

CONCLUSIONS

Democratising civic Scotland has always been one of the main arguments put forward by proponents of a Scottish parliament. So the accountability of the Scottish Qualifications Authority was a natural issue for the parliament to engage with, as were the wider question about how policy is made. Many campaigners for a parliament had believed that civic Scotland – the leaders of Scottish institutions – had become insufferably complacent. In education, the key culprits in this regard were alleged to be the inspectorate, the civil servants in the Education Department, and the plethora of quangos and committees that advise them. It was not usually claimed that these people were incompetent or corrupt, but rather that their world was too inward-looking to be able to renovate the education system successfully.

The inspectorate has largely been invisible to people outwith education itself, and yet anyone who has ever analysed any aspect of Scottish educational policy-making has concluded that it is the key group. The inspectors have always played a more important role in providing policy advice than in England and Wales, and this difference was intensified when most of the English and

Welsh inspectorate was privatised in the mid-1990s. The Scottish inspectors were remarkably successful in resisting this, retaining their roles of recommending policy changes, overseeing the implementation of change, commissioning research on how successful that implementation has been, and inspecting schools' and colleges' work in carrying out the changes. Retaining these roles ensured that the Scottish inspectorate remained at the heart of policy-making. It was hardly surprising, then, that its role in Higher Still should be so insistently questioned, not just after the crisis in August 2000, but right back to 1994 and before.

But the immediate political context, too, helped to shape the debate that followed the crisis. Although appearing to be about the minutiae of party politics and about the particular personalities of the people who spoke for the parties on education, the political arguments actually raised much deeper issues which transcend those particular individuals, and outlast their tenure of their posts. It is always thus with politics. What can appear trivial and personal actually reflects the key underlying tensions in a society. During August and September 2000 Sam Galbraith, Nicola Sturgeon and Brian Monteith were expressing some fundamental questions about accountability, about the status of civic Scotland, about the tensions between élites and civil society, and about the role of educational traditions in sustaining a sense of nationhood. It is the capacity to focus these kinds of debate that makes politics ultimately a noble task, and makes a national parliament the primary means by which a nation reflects on its history and future.

CHAPTER 6

The Parliamentary Inquiries

The scale of the crisis in August 2000 made it inevitable that the Scottish parliament would be drawn in, not just because of the attacks on the education minister which were coming from the SNP and the Tories, but also because of the role which the parliamentary committees are intended to play. The Consultative Steering Group of 1998, whose report had set out the working practices of the parliament, had made the committees' scrutinising role abundantly clear. Among their many tasks, committees, it said, should have the capacity:

- to consider and report on the policy and administration of the Scottish Administration;
- to conduct inquiries into such matters or issues as the parliament may require.

Two committees were involved here. The main one was that responsible for Education, Culture and Sport: its remit covers the whole of school education, and so it was the natural first place to which questions were referred. But the Enterprise and Lifelong Learning committee also had a role, partly because Higher Still was being used by further education colleges as well as schools, and partly because, rather bizarrely, the responsibility for the SQA as a quango then lay with the corresponding minister, Henry McLeish, and not with the schools minister, Sam Galbraith.

The Education committee moved swiftly. When its convener, the Labour MSP Mary Mulligan, mooted an inquiry over the weekend immediately after the crisis broke, no one objected. The terms of reference were agreed on 6 September, shortly after the parliament resumed sitting after the summer recess, and evidence was solicited that would allow the inquiry to:

- review the impact on school pupils, and on their future prospects, of the performance of the SQA in issuing qualifications certificates this year;
- identify the causes of the difficulties encountered this year, including aspects of the marking process, problems with administration of the SQA, and the implementation of Higher Still;
- make recommendations on how such difficulties may be avoided in future, and on how confidence in this year's results and next year's results can be restored.

Ms Mulligan said on several occasions, in public, that the inquiry had to be impartial, and genuinely independent of the government. The committee contains 11 members, five of whom are from the Labour Party, two from the Liberal Democrats, three from the SNP (including Nicola Sturgeon and her successor as education spokesperson, Mike Russell), and one Tory (Brian Monteith). There was thus a government majority, but not a Labour majority. The committee was serviced by a clerk and a specialist adviser, Hamish Long (a retired chief executive of the Examination Board).

Although the Lifelong Learning committee did go ahead with a more limited inquiry into the accountability aspects, there was an amicable agreement to leave all the educational issues (including for colleges) to the Education committee inquiry.

The inquiries have each provoked two streams of evidence, much of which has already been used throughout this book. One was in written form; the other was in the public sessions that took evidence orally. This chapter summarises the main themes to have emerged from this evidence, and illustrates what witnesses had to say. But the role of the inquiries was not only to solicit evidence; it was also to make the issues public. Some of the most telling moments at the inquiries were during oral exchanges, and a few of these are summarised here too. The purpose of sifting all this evidence is to look for a consensus view on the problems. The analysis in this book has sought to provide that, looking beyond the official versions to what teachers and others have been saying for nearly a decade. But is the analysis offered here a plausible way of viewing the events of August 2000? The chapter deals mainly with evidence to the Education committee, and, unless otherwise stated, evidence cited here was given to that inquiry. But some reference is also made to the Lifelong Learning committee's work in connection with the question of accountability.

BACKGROUND ISSUES

The first set of points made to the inquiry concerns the whole history of Higher Still. None of the witnesses apart from those attached in some way to the Education Department or the SQA believed that the problems lay only with the administration of data in school session 1999–2000 and of results in summer 2000. Teachers had been warning about the practical problems of implementation for several years. For example, here is how the history was summarised before the committee on 4 October by George MacBride, convener of the education committee of the EIS: 'First, I think that there is general support for the principles that underpin the Higher Still programme. Secondly, there are concerns about certain aspects of that programme, and in particular internal assessment. Thirdly, among all the teaching unions, considerable anxiety was caused by the perception that Higher Still was being imposed for political reasons and without adequate resourcing. Fourthly – this is perhaps the most important aspect of the imposition – there was a strong feeling among many teachers that they were excluded from any real debate, either about the principles or the practicalities of implementation. The reasons for that feeling relate to the culture within which we operated in Scottish education for much of the 1990s. The feeling led to the view that Higher Still was a political mantra to be pursued.'

These views were echoed by representatives of other teacher unions, and also by Alex Easton, rector of Falkirk High School: 'There was an overambitious push on schools from the Higher Still Development Unit and [the inspectorate]. We were perceived as conservative if we tried to suggest that we move forward at a reasonable pace, as happened with Standard Grade. If at public meetings we said that we ought to ca' canny and think things through, the response was often very sarcastic.'

So far as data management was concerned, the committee was

told that schools had been warning of problems throughout session 1999–2000, but had been unable to have their concerns taken seriously because no one in authority would admit that the problems were likely to lead to a disaster. Ann Hill, speaking on behalf of the Scottish School Board Association, quoted a letter she had received from Banchory Academy in March 2000 (and which was also submitted in writing to the inquiry): 'The print-out we have received has been checked so far only for Standard Grade pupils. We have found errors in every single subject, most noticeably in maths – 80 not accounted for, English 25 missing and other subjects in smaller numbers. I heard anecdotal evidence of a girl in another school being listed for 17 Highers in 16 of which the school does not present candidates.' The written submission from the School Board Association provided several other examples. Mrs Hill commented: 'That is the kind of evidence that led us to worry that children would not be registered.'

Judith Gillespie, by now development manager of the Scottish Parent Teacher Council, reported that she had frequently heard concerns expressed about data management. Pressed by Labour committee member Ken Macintosh to explain why witnesses could not give documented evidence of these concerns, she pointed out that 'people did not collect such evidence at the time, because they were not aware that the issue was significant'. She and others on the Higher Still Liaison Group had distrusted the inspectorate report in February 2000 which claimed that the implementation of Higher Still was going extremely well, but, not themselves being able to assess the likely effect of these problems, they could take the matter no further. Ms Gillespie's point that no one was willing to treat the warnings seriously is reinforced when we note that Mrs Hill was also a member of the SQA board. It has been claimed by the minister that she did not report her evidence to any meeting of the board, but the fact that it was given front-page treatment in *The Herald* in April 2000 should have brought it to the attention of the SQA management and the Education Department. Either the significance of what she was saying – or of what Ms Gillespie was saying at meetings of the Liaison Group –

was not appreciated, which would bring into question the competence of the relevant managers, or it was ignored because Higher Still had to be forced through at all costs. Neither interpretation casts a very positive light on the people in charge. In the words of Margaret Nicol, president of the EIS, 'During the first year of implementation, we found that [the inspectorate], quite rightly, picked up the positive view of what was happening in schools, but seemed to be failing to pick up the problems and the more negative aspects, particularly in relation to internal assessment.'

George MacBride was not the only witness to mention the problems of internal assessment. He expanded on these: 'The pressures on young people to pass those assessments, the need to reassess where a young person failed to achieve a cut-off score, and the knock-on effects on teaching and learning caused substantial difficulties, which must be addressed in reviewing Higher Still.'

A particularly clear summary of the effect on students came from Janette Moore, chairwoman of Uddingston Grammar School Board, speaking on 9 October: 'Other points of concern that parents raised with me concerned the number of internal assessments and the stress that these occasioned. Parents also cited the fact that the unit tests did not always bear any relation to the end examination and mentioned the apparent increase in work that was required in comparison with that which was required for the old Highers. Some pupils feel that what they are doing now is sitting courses for the sake of passing exams and that there is no enjoyment in studying subjects that they want to learn about. They are working only to pass exams and tests.'

Likewise, Elspeth Banks, headteacher of Strathaven Academy, said: 'All secondary-school pupils in Scotland are used to assessments. In the course of study in their Higher year, all pupils are used to end-of-topic check tests and assessment. They are for formative, as opposed to summative, judgement. That was the difference this year. Although the end-of-topic check tests were pursued, the unit tests were formal. That placed an additional burden on our candidates.'

The union representatives felt that part of the problem lay with the speed of implementation. David Eaglesham, general secretary of the Scottish Secondary Teachers Association, said on 4 October: 'It is quite clear that there was a political determination that Higher Still should go ahead, that it should go ahead in a particular way and in a particular time frame, and that nothing should stop it, least of all genuine reporting by the profession of serious problems of implementation. We made the point repeatedly that no teacher in Scotland would have benefited by a penny from delaying Higher Still. However, we were still told that we were putting our narrow interests ahead of the interests of the pupils. We said repeatedly and in public that the unions and the members whom we represent were putting the interests of the pupils first.' And, he concluded in response to questioning on the effects of the timetable, 'There was haste that eventually proved to be damaging.'

On 9 October Ken Anderson, vice-chairman of the school board at Strathaven Academy, summed up the effects of the speed of implementation on students: 'The [Education] committee should consider whether it might be better to delay implementation of Higher Still for a year, rather than introduce something that is half baked. The bottom line is that we, as parents, feel that it is unacceptable that our kids should be treated as guinea pigs at a vital time of their lives.'

The point was also made in the written evidence, and during the hearings, that there was an absence of any well-developed philosophical rationale for Higher Still. In this respect, the most impressive paper submitted to the committee was from the Association of Directors of Education in Scotland. The paper is cogent, far removed from the dead bureaucratic prose that has emerged from much educational management in the last couple of decades. As we saw in Chapter 4, the submission had pertinent points to make about many aspects of the Higher Still programme – assessment, moderation, management, workload of both teachers and students, and accountability. But it also addressed the question of the 'philosophical underpinning'. It pointed out that: 'The philosophical underpinning of the Higher Still programme never received the iterative examination that was recognised as being necessary at the formative stage of the programme's development in 1996. The failure to undertake such an examination created many of the core conditions which have led to a number of the major difficulties which have been observed over the last few months. It can be argued that they represent as much a philosophical as an administrative and bureaucratic failure.'

The submission then mentioned the big philosophical issues which the directors felt were never debated. They noted that there was no discussion of whether, and on what basis, it was possible to unify academic and vocational qualification systems. There was no consultation at all on the principles of assessment, 'the details being embedded in the proposals for individual subjects': 'In consequence, the major debate which should have taken place not merely on the principles of the new assessment régime, but on its practical operation, failed to materialise.'

None of the official submissions to the inquiry would lead us to doubt the judgement that basic issues of philosophy seem rarely to have crossed the minds of the technocrats in charge. For example, when Ian Jenkins, a Liberal Democrat member of the committee, asked John Elvidge, head of the Education Department, about the consequences of the 'Scottish Vocational Education Council philosophy entering the exam system', he chose to reply entirely in terms of statistics on the number of unit assessments that candidates had to undertake. Similarly, in his evidence on 9 October, Douglas Osler chose not to address any issues concerning the underlying philosophy of the reform, although it has to be said also that he was not pressed on this, since committee members concentrated almost entirely on the responsibility for the chaos surrounding the issuing of exam certificates.

EFFECTS IN THE YEAR 2000

The committee's concern with immediate events was understandable, given how their inquiry had arisen, but also because most of the written and oral submissions dwelt on that. The most graphic evidence came from school students who appeared before the committee in Hamilton on 9 October (a hearing outside Edinburgh of the type which the Consultative Steering Group had been keen to encourage in its 1998 report on how the parliament should operate). The opening summary from Lewis MacKinnon, a sixth-year student at Uddingston Grammar School, would be recognised by thousands of students across Scotland, and is worth quoting in full for its succinct eloquence: 'When 10 August came, my results did not. I waited but they had still not come by the late post. I was concerned, so I phoned the school to find out whether it had received notification. However, it did not know what had happened, so I phoned the SQA helpline, which I had seen mentioned on television. I was told to phone the school again and then phone the helpline back. The school still did not know anything; it was in the same position as me.

'I therefore phoned the SQA helpline again. The people there reluctantly said that they could give me the results via the phone, but would prefer it if I waited until my results came. I was anxious, as members will understand, so I asked them to tell me the results. They went through each result, but omitted my physics one. I told them that I had sat Higher physics and asked what had happened with that. They said that they did not have any record of it. I was concerned, because I had done quite well in physics and hoped to study it further in sixth year. I let the school know and waited.

'The next day the results finally came in the post. The format of the results is that your overall Higher awards are on the front; a more complicated form gives you a breakdown of how you were awarded them, including the unit tests. When I read through it, it turned out that only two of the three unit tests that I had passed had been recorded. I had got an A in my external assessment – the exam that you sit in May or June. I had passed all my unit tests and got an A for the exam, so I expected an A. However, there was no record of me sitting the third unit test. It had been sent away with the rest of the information.

'I let the school know and received notification in September that there had been a problem and I would get the result eventually.'

Not surprisingly, given this, the students reported that they experienced a great deal of stress. Alan Burns, a student from the same school, said that 'In the weeks before your results come out, the tension builds up and you get more nervous. On the day, you just want to get your results and get it over with; afterwards, you can relax, but I could not because my results did not come. I am still highly strung and worried about what is going to happen.'

This, remember, was a full two months after the results were meant to have appeared. Another student, Jennifer Irvine of Earnock High School, reported on the stress induced by thinking that she was alone with the problem: 'I thought it was just me. I was not aware of the problems the media had been talking about, as I had been on holiday and had got home the night before.'

None of the witnesses would have made light of the trauma which these young people were put through. But there would have been disagreement over how well events were handled from 10 August – when the results were due to be issued – onwards. It was clear from the evidence presented on 9 October by students, parents and teachers that part of the problem had been a lack of official recognition that there really was a crisis. Proper political leadership sometimes involves simply acknowledging people's fears. The story of the ensuing few weeks was of repeated assurances by people in authority that matters were not as bad as was being claimed, and then of these assurances being proven to be unwarranted shortly after. For example, in its written submission, East Lothian Council noted that the refusal initially to accept the scale of the crisis added to students' worries: 'The minister's dismissal [on 11 August] of anyone casting doubts on all certificates as being "totally irresponsible" was unhelpful.'

Examples of other claims that were initially dismissed as without foundation were the necessity of suspending university selection procedures, the scale of appeals that would be likely to ensue, the inevitability of some students losing a university place, certainly of their choice and possibly altogether, and the rate at which successful appeals would be running. All of these have turned out to be as serious as claimed by the most severe criticisms of the SQA that were being made during August.

If we needed proof that the evidence presented by the Lanark-shire students on 9 October was typical of what the committee would have found had it visited any other area of Scotland, and that there was a great deal of complacency in high places during August, we need look only at the rate of success among the urgent appeals that had to be dealt with for students hoping to go on to higher education in autumn 2000. The success rate, at about 40 per cent, was actually substantially higher than in most recent years: according to the SQA's annual reports in 1998 and 1999, the rate of successful appeals at Higher grade has ranged recently from 41 per cent in 1994 to 28 per cent in 1998 and 32 per cent in 1999. If the whole furore had indeed been alarmist and irresponsible, as was alleged by people in authority in August, an unprecedented proportion of the appeals would have been found to have been unjustified, and so the rate of successful appeals would have dropped sharply; but in fact it has risen, and so the concerns raised have been vindicated.

The entire episode was then judged by several witnesses to have placed grave doubts on the SQA quality assurance pro-cedures. George MacBride of the EIS summed up what seemed to have gone wrong by pointing to what needed to be done: 'There must be a clear statement that the timing of the exam diet and the announcement of the results – matters within the control of the Scottish Executive rather than the SQA – will allow for marking and subsequent and accompanying quality-assurance procedures to take place. That must include the more senior markers con-sidering how markers have performed and the concordance pro-cedures through computer programmes. Sufficient time for those checks and balances must be built into the timescale. That is a first and important step.'

The 'concordance procedures' are (as we saw in Chapter 1) the routine means by which the results on students' certificates are made broadly consistent with what their school expects of them. This can be thought of as a quality-control procedure on the grounds that teachers know their students' abilities better than anyone else in the education system, although to interpret these in that way requires that schools and teachers be trusted. There

was good reason to have that trust because, as John Kelly of
another union, the NASUWT, said: 'For many years, schools have
been told that they must be accurate in their estimates, for the
very good reason that if the child underperforms on the day, they
can be accorded the performance of which they were thought to
be capable.' He pointed out, however, that that required good
feedback about exam standards from the SQA to teachers, which
did not seem to be forthcoming in 2000.

Quality assurance was another matter on which complacency
was abundantly in evidence in August 2000. As we saw in Chapter
1, on the BBC Scotland debate on 22 August, the interim chief
executive of the SQA, Bill Morton, said that the normal quality-
assurance procedures of the SQA had been in place. Only later did
it emerge that the concordancy checks – one crucial part of
quality assurance – were in fact absent. The concordancy checks
were not carried out for any of the Higher Still courses in 2000,
purportedly on the grounds that teachers had no track record of
predicting students' performance in these new exams (an objection that had not interfered with the use of concordances or their
predecessors when Standard Grade was introduced, or when
major revisions in the old Higher syllabuses and exams had taken
place earlier in the 1990s). This absence was known on 22 August,
as Ron Tuck, former chief executive of the SQA, implicitly admitted to the inquiry when he appeared on 4 October.

There were also comments in the submissions on the lack of
moderation (a point that was discussed in Chapter 4). There was
at least some evidence that the administration of marking had not
been as rigorous as in previous years. For example, there were
instances of markers being asked to take on extra scripts at the
very last minute, of teachers being asked to mark scripts for
students in their own schools, of the nominally independent
inspectors marking scripts, and of some scripts being marked by
probationer teachers.

And there were several suggestions that, given what had
happened in 2000, the only way to restore faith in the quality of
the exams was by making marked scripts available to students, as
was done in England and Wales for the first time in 2000. There

was some rather patronising resistance to this in the written evidence submitted by the Education Department. For example, at a regular meeting of the liaison committee of the Department and the SQA on 8 February 2000, a report was received on the successful policy of returning scripts that was operating in New Zealand, and it was noted that the change of policy in England and Wales may make for irresistible pressure to do the same in Scotland. But, said the minutes, 'it seems likely that return of scripts would encourage complaints or queries'. The idea that this might be the whole point in a more open democracy seems to have been missed.

The matter was taken up at the inquiry by the Tory education spokesman, Brian Monteith, questioning Andrew Shanks, principal teacher of English in Montrose Academy (and head of one of the few departments that had implemented the new English and Communication exam in 2000): 'Do you support the idea that scripts from appeals – not all exams – should be returned to schools as a means of determining whether the initial marking of papers and appeals scripts, or the contributory factors of sitting Higher Still, have led to so many students' dissatisfaction with their marks?'

Mr Shanks was sceptical, in terms quite similar to those expressed at the official meeting in February: 'At the moment teachers want scripts to be returned, because they are frustrated and angry and want some evidence to prove either that their expectations for candidates were not met in the exam, or that they were right. However, I can see the SQA's problem. If every teacher disputes every mark in every exam, we could end up with quite a debacle. Although returning scripts seems like a great idea, it might turn out to provide less clarity and transparency than we suppose. I would not choose that option.'

This view was endorsed by other union representatives who were present, but Mr Monteith was not persuaded, on the grounds that only by returning scripts could the 'large degree of mistrust of the marking and the appeals process' be dealt with.

And the president of the EIS, Margaret Nicol, gave a less categorical reply: 'I do not object to commenting on the situation south of the border, where scripts were returned in a planned way. The decision was taken to return exam scripts and the marking process took account of that decision.'

It is unlikely that this issue will go away. One assiduous parent, Liz Walker of Kilbirnie (a former activist in the Conservative Party), had found out from the SQA that scripts are destroyed by the February of the year following the date of the exam, apart from a small, randomly selected sample kept on file for future checking of exam and marking standards. She pointed out (in correspondence with me) that this made checking the validity of the results for any particular candidate a matter of extreme urgency, but that, in the absence of a right to see scripts, individual students or their parents were not able to force checking to take place. The forthcoming Freedom of Information Act might change the situation, as might the European Convention on Human Rights, but in the meantime parents felt powerless. In any case, so far as the disputed results of year 2000 were concerned, not destroying the scripts would seem a prudent option.

Probably the most long-lasting effect of the disaster was felt to be the consequences for the reputation of the exams and of Scottish education as a whole. It had already been found by the media that trust in the exams had plummeted. The *Sunday Times* of 27 August reported a poll of headteachers in which 75 per cent said they were dissatisfied with the standard of marking, 14 per cent wanted internal assessment abandoned altogether, and a further 34 per cent wanted some changes to it. (As we saw earlier, the EIS had already voted in June 1999 for an end to all the formal unit assessments.) In *The Herald* on 2 September, a poll of people in Scotland as a whole found that 68 per cent did not 'believe the exam results can be trusted as accurate and reliable'. In November, one large employer (Scottish Widows) annouced that they would not be using Higher Still results for recruitment.

In its written submission, East Lothian Council reported that among young people the 'SQA is now largely regarded with derision'. Certainly distrust was clearly in evidence at the inquiry's hearing in Hamilton on 9 October. The students gave their overall verdicts in reply to a question from Mike Russell of the SNP:

'Presumably you will all have to take examinations in future, as you are locked into the system. What comes to your minds when you think about that after your experience this year?'

The replies left no room for doubt. Jennifer Irvine, of Earnock High School, said: 'I do not feel that confident in the system.' Namita Veer Nayyar of Hamilton Grammar School said: 'It is a question of trust. Can we trust what we are going to be given when we sit exams?'

No exam system can survive these levels of mistrust among teachers, local authorities, employers, the general public and students.

Nevertheless, there remained a faith that the education system was basically fair. When pressed on her plans by the deputy convener, the Labour MSP Cathy Peattie, Namita Veer Nayyar showed a continuing belief that – despite everything – the system would provide an assessment of her talents in the ways that it had done for her predecessors for over a century: 'My UCAS form has to be sent in because I am hoping to do dentistry at Glasgow University. I have spoken to the department a lot as I am interested in the course. I was told that C passes were discounted. That means that only my three A passes and one B pass will be taken into account. The university wants me to get a B in a chemistry Certificate of Sixth Year Studies this year. That will make sixth year another hard year.'

Cathy Peattie: 'But you will have a bash and see if you can pick it up.'

Namita Veer Nayyar: 'Yes, because I really want to do dentistry. I will have to work hard at it.'

That students could continue to believe that, if they work hard, they will be rewarded suggests that the underlying quality of the education system has not been brought into question. Whether that moderately optimistic inference is valid will, of course, be clear only with the passage of a great deal of time.

EXPLANATIONS

The evidence also offered plenty of suggestions for what had gone wrong. Without doubt there had been maladministration at the

SQA. One way of looking at it was detailed in the written submission from Bill Morton, interim chief executive, who seems to have treated his own inquiry in much the same way as if he had been looking into the work of any private-sector business. (Much the same conclusions were reached by the report which the Scottish government commissioned from management consultants Deloitte and Touche.) According to Mr Morton, there had been no proper estimation in advance of the scale of the operation that would be required to deal with certificates; planning and preparation were poor. There was hardly any risk assessment, and there were few 'designed-in checks and balances' (even though, as we saw, there was plenty of confidence that all contingencies had been covered). Management information was 'not robust', which presumably means was unreliable and therefore wrong. Data received from schools was lost or incorrectly entered into the SQA's computers, as everyone knew. Management structures were cumbersome, and accountability was lacking, although Mr Morton also criticised the tendency to make decisions by committee, which in fact is often the way in which publicly accountable organisations operate. There was 'a lack of customer focus', commercial language that even the founding Act had eschewed (referring instead to 'users').

None of this came as any surprise to anyone who had been observing or experiencing the effect of the SQA, which included all those who gave evidence to the inquiry. The official line from the SQA, the Education Department and the inspectorate had clearly been agreed. In the words of Ron Tuck, in his written submission, 'the crucial flaw lay in the management of data'. Nothing he said in his oral presentations contradicted that, and it is likely to be the case that that is what he and his senior colleagues sincerely believed. After all, they had an organisation to run, and – by summer 2000 – were doing what they could, and were in no position to question how they and their organisation had got there. As he said on 4 October: 'The duty of the leadership of an organisation is not to get bogged down in despondency. You must lift your staff. You must project an image of confidence – but not undue confidence because the staff are well informed. Our tone through that period was, "Yes, we understand the concerns. There are real difficulties. This is what we are doing about it. Let us get ahead and do it."' But all this proves is that summer 2000 was much too late a stage at which to try to sort things out.

One of the quaintly naive things about how they did get there – even leaving aside all the educational questions about Higher Still – was the faith that was shown in large new computer systems working correctly the first time round. There was no particular reason, apart from politics, why Higher Still had to start in the same year as the new systems. They could have been tried out on the old Highers, with the old systems running as a back-up in case things did go wrong. There have been several recent similar problems in the public sector – notably over passports. One of the questions which the inquiry kept coming back to was this: why did the information-technology advisers to the SQA and the Education Department not seem to share in this common culture? Are the personnel of these organisations too inward-looking, too isolated from mainstream debate about good management practice? Jack Greig, formerly operations manager at the SQA, said in his evidence on 25 October that no one in his department had any professional data-processing qualifications: they hoped to learn from experience. And, for all Mr Morton's bringing of his commercial experience to the SQA, the question about competence in managing a large new computer system was not put in his evidence. When Mike Russell asked him on 9 October, 'Do you understand what went wrong with the computer system?', he chose to interpret that as a question about software and hardware: 'I made clear that the data-management problem is essentially a behavioural thing. The SQA did not get that right. It is not the same as there being problems with the technology or the hardware.'

Mr Russell then pressed him on his intended review: 'Does the process include an examination of the qualifications and experience of those who head information technology in the SQA? The committee has discussed the fact that IT did not seem to be given its proper place in the management structure and that there were people in charge of IT who had limited experience of writing programs. Will that be changed as part of the solution?'

To this, Mr Morton replied in a manner that suggests that the lesson had not been learnt that the interaction between human beings and machines is precisely where large, complex computer systems tend to break down: 'We will examine that, but I have not encountered any direct evidence that would suggest that the in-house capability was failing in the sense that you imply. Clearly there were instances of poor project management in the sense that user specifications for the software were being thought up at the same time as the software was being created. There is clear evidence that the software was not adequately tested. We need to think about the software as part of the planning for next year. If we believe that we need a capacity and capability that we do not have, we will procure it.'

The problem is that you can't 'procure' a workplace culture. That the SQA culture was woefully inadequate was shown by Mr Greig's evidence on 25 October. For example, software had been delivered a matter of days before it had to be used, and a third of his staff were summarily moved to another department by the chief executive Ron Tuck.

ACCOUNTABILITY

The final broad area in which comments were made to the inquiry is in connection with accountability, and here the parallel inquiry by the Lifelong Learning committee is also relevant. Over and over again, the witnesses representing teachers and parents pointed to the key role of the inspectorate in overseeing Higher Still, and therefore in having ultimate responsibility for the policy. This was put clearly on 4 October by John Kelly, convener of the education committee of the NASUWT, one of the smaller unions. Referring to Brian Wilson's comments on the lack of information which he received from the inspectorate when he was education minister, he said: 'There was a reluctance on the part of Her Majesty's inspectors of schools and, possibly, the Higher Still Development Unit to give ministers messages that they might not have wanted to hear.'

He then commented more generally: 'The problem is not with personalities in the inspectorate but with the role of the inspectorate as it has been constituted in the past ten years. In our evidence on the Standards in Scotland's Schools Act 2000, we pointed out that the inspectorate is now both the generator of policy and the policeman of policy, which cannot be right. If the inspectorate is pushing Higher Still – and it could be something else tomorrow – is it the best-suited body to listen to and represent the problems that might occur in implementation?'

Several witnesses pointed out that – as we have seen – the inspectorate had been closely involved in monitoring the SQA from autumn 1999 until summer 2000, a role that indicates the responsibility which the inspectorate felt it had for the new examination system. At no point in either the written or the oral evidence from the Education Department was it suggested that the inspectors' intense involvement over the summer of 2000 was anything other than perfectly normal and proper. For example, on 27 September, Fiona Mcleod, an SNP member of the committee, pressed the head of the Department, John Elvidge, on what they had done to check up on the assurances that they had received from the SQA. The full exchange is:

Fiona McLeod: 'I wonder what it takes to set alarm bells ringing in the Scottish Executive. Throughout the questioning, we have heard that you never thoroughly checked out the reassurances that you were given. What does it take to make the Scottish Executive say, "Let's investigate a bit further and ensure that we are getting the right answers"?'

John Elvidge: 'That is a bit of a cheap shot. I am not sure what your definition of thoroughly checking something out is.'

Fiona McLeod: 'We want to hear your definition.'

John Elvidge: 'I have given you at some length my definition of the processes that it is possible to follow to try to check that something that one has been told is true. A judgement must be made about whether individual questions are central to the issues. Throughout the process, we discussed with the SQA a wide range of emerging issues that might have been a source of anxiety. We pursued each issue in a way that was proportionate to the risk that it appeared to pose to the outcome. We followed a proportionate process of checking with the SQA.'

The revealing thing about this last answer is its assumptions and what it does not say. It assumes – correctly – that it is constitutionally and legally proper for the Department to be closely involved with the operations of the quango. It does not raise any questions about interference or any such matter: under such emergency conditions, the Department may do what it wants. This is no surprise after what we have seen about the inspectorate's role in policy-making. It was so intimately involved in the development of Higher Still that it was bound to take a close interest in how it was working during its first year.

Part of the problem seems to have been that, despite this, the means by which the views of the Department and the inspectorate were communicated to the board of the SQA were not working very well. The Lifelong Learning committee took evidence from another pair of quangos, the Scottish Higher Education Funding Council and the Scottish Further Education Funding Council, to provide a point of comparison with what happened at the SQA. On 29 September, the chief executive of both councils, John Sizer, said that a part of his duties was to pass on to his councils information about all important contacts which he and his staff had with the relevant government department: 'There is no formal liaison between the Scottish Executive and either of the funding councils, although we have regular contact at various levels. When I am involved in discussions with [the Department of Enterprise and Lifelong Learning] on matters that concern the responsibilities of the council, I report back automatically. Such discussions frequently lead to a communication from the Executive either to me or to the chairman of one of the bodies.'

We can then contrast this with evidence received by the same committee about how poorly informed the board of the SQA were about the developing problems with data management during session 1999–2000. At the board meeting on 23 September 1999, members were told about the progress of the new awards processing system (for issuing certificates), and 'it was agreed that board members should be kept informed between meetings of any major issue of concern in connection with implementation of the awards processing system'.

Information passed on between meetings is not minuted. At the next meeting, on 9 December, a few difficulties were noted, but 'reported difficulties notwithstanding, the SQA had received [examination] entries – and indeed some results [of unit assessments] – electronically and the indications were that remaining software suppliers would have working systems available for [schools and colleges] by the end of the year'.

That optimism may be contrasted with the alarm that was already being raised in the inspectorate by the reports of data-management problems. As we saw in Chapter 4, by the time of that December meeting of the board, a meeting had already taken place on 23 November between Neil MacGowan of the SQA and the inspector Carolyn Hutchinson. By any measure, this was an important event clearly relating to the item on the agenda for the December board. There is no evidence that it was even mentioned, in stark contrast to what appears to be the practice in the Higher and Further Education Funding Councils.

This complacency at board level continued right through the school session. At the meeting on 23 March 2000, no mention was made of the increasingly urgent approaches that (as we also saw in Chapter 4) SQA senior managers were receiving from the Education Department, nor of the deep concerns that teachers' and parents' leaders had raised at the February meeting of the Higher Still Liaison Group, nor, indeed, of the warnings which the SQA's own staff were giving to their senior management team. And then, at the meeting on 22 June, the chief executive Ron Tuck was reported as giving this reassurance: 'Data remained a difficulty, with much still to be submitted as well as many queries requiring resolution. However, [schools and colleges] were being encouraged to submit data as soon as possible and named school contacts were being sought for the resolution of any remaining queries during the July period.'

That little word 'any' betrays the complacency, but what is even more bizarre is the contrast between that minute and what Ron Tuck said in his own written evidence to the committee, which shows that management knew the situation to be far worse: 'By the end of June, we became aware that we had significant problems with the management of data. From then onwards, meetings with Scottish Executive officials were held on a weekly basis. We informed them of progress in respect of marker recruitment, software development, implementation of post-examination processes, and chasing missing data. The problem of missing data ultimately proved to be critical.'

These contacts with the Executive – which were already in train by the end of June, as the Education Department's submission to the Education Committee makes clear – were not reported to the board.

Ron Tuck takes a different view of the seriousness of all this. He acknowledged in his written evidence that 'the SQA board and Scottish Executive could act only on the basis of information provided by SQA senior management'. He said that he and his colleagues were 'not fully aware' of the scale of the problems. It is not clear how this can be reconciled with the quite urgent awareness that the inspectorate seemed to have. Mr Tuck also said, in his oral evidence, that 'members of the board asked the right kind of questions', which he defined as 'the kind of questions that I would have asked had I been a board member'. Maybe so, but they do not appear to have asked for the kind of information that John Sizer routinely provides to his Funding Councils. The SQA board did not seem to ask for information about contacts with the Education Department, and the senior management seems not to have volunteered it.

In the light of these various points about accountability – either of the SQA itself, or of the inspectorate – several witnesses also raised more general points about how policy is made. The Association of Directors of Education put the point most forcefully: 'The failings in the examination system this year and the events which led up to them demonstrate clearly the shortcomings of current mechanisms for promoting change in Scottish education.'

They then list the key failings: too much complexity in Higher Still, as designed by the Development Unit (and, through them, by the inspectorate); the lack of proper consultation on fundamentals; and the reluctance to respond flexibly to concerns that were raised during implementation. They conclude that these failings all arose 'from over-centralisation and a lack of accountability to the majority of legitimate stakeholders'. And so 'if the new constitutional dispensation in Scotland is to bring higher quality and more responsive public services, these issues need to be tackled urgently'.

CONCLUSIONS

Some conclusions that may be reached from the mass of evidence are discussed in the remaining two chapters, but we can draw some preliminary lessons here about the role of the inquiries. They achieved four main things, and had two drawbacks.

Their first role was simply to provide a platform. They agreed almost without demur that all their work should be in public, and the resulting sessions gave an opportunity for all the anxieties of the summer, and anger about Higher Still over many years, to be given a dignified airing. At the same time, the informality that has come to characterise the proceedings of the parliament must have helped many of the witnesses to speak out. It was clear from the evidence taken in Hamilton that the students, parents and teachers there were made to feel that their worries were being taken seriously, and their eloquence testifies to that ethos having produced the desired effect. Much credit for this must go to the convener, Labour's Mary Mulligan, whose discreet and sympathetic chairing could hardly be more different from the confrontational style that politicians are often criticised for. But all the committee members picked up on this, and some – notably Labour member Cathy Peattie – showed a real concern for the witnesses' welfare. A similar tone was set in the Lifelong Learning committee by its deputy convener, the Conservative Annabel Goldie, and then by its new convener, the SNP's Alex Neil, when he took over in October. There is a time and place for confrontational politics, but it is not in inquiries of this sort, and the committees acquitted themselves well.

The second role the inquiries played – especially that by the Education committee – was to provide a focus for public worries. The importance of this should not be underestimated. In the absence of a national debate on matters of urgent public concern, feelings of powerlessness and cynicism flourish. Providing such a way of concentrating minds has always been one of the most cogent cultural arguments for a Scottish parliament. All through August 2000, people were thinking about the prospect of a parliamentary inquiry, and many bodies were preparing to make submissions. The evidence is then available electronically through the excellent Official Record, and through the assiduous work of the Scottish Parliament Information Centre, collating all the written submissions and scanning them into electronic form. This particular episode has then been much better and more swiftly documented than most previous major incidents in Scottish education, and so the opportunities for society as a whole to learn from it are greater. This is the parliament acting as a kind of clearing house.

The third achievement was to provide, at best, rigorous questioning. Never before have people of the seniority of the head of the inspectorate or the civil service head of the Education Department been subjected to such sustained interrogation in public. The members of the committee mostly rose to that challenge for at least some of the time, especially when they insisted on Douglas Osler returning to give evidence on his own: at his first appearance, he had remained mostly silent beside John Elvidge.

And the fourth achievement arose from that – beginning to create a culture of openness in Scottish public affairs. When senior figures in Scottish education know that they may have to account for their actions in front of inquiries of this sort, they will take greater care to be able to justify what they do. Where there are failings, this clarity will then make it easier for politicians to decide where reforms have to take place. By empowering less powerful people, the parliament can also show that part of the process of openness is making sure that the channels of communication and accountability within Scottish institutions – such as within the education system – are working effectively. Sometimes the first point of accountability is not between politicians and the specialists in a highly complex public service, but rather between the senior people and the less influential within the same service, such as school teachers. The parliament can facilitate these processes, and the Education committee's inquiry began on that task.

Nevertheless, two caveats to these positive conclusions have to be entered. The first is that the questioning was not always as penetrating as it could have been. This probably arose mainly because of a certain diffidence on the part of the MSPs, faced with the experience and technical knowledge of their senior witnesses. For example, at no point was any witness tackled on the question of assessment philosophy, and yet, as we have seen in Chapter 4, that has been one of the burning issues of contention in Higher Still. There were plenty of questions about the sheer burden of assessment, but nothing much about what assessment is intended to achieve. The lack of such questioning is hardly surprising, since it requires an expertise that only professional educational-ists would tend to have. The Liberal Democrat Ian Jenkins, a former teacher, did ask some relevant questions of John Elvidge, but, as we saw earlier in this chapter, they were answered bureau-cratically, and the philosophical issues were not pursued. Probably the only way to resolve this kind of problem in the long run is to have a much expanded specialist staff available to the committees. Excellent though the parliament's information centre is, including the committee clerks, they cannot hope to be experts in all the specialist topics that the committees cover, and so some structured way needs to be found to bring in outside help. Simply attaching one expert adviser to the committee for a brief period of time is not enough. It has to be said, though, that providing a proper specialist service would cost money: that is one of the necessary prices of an effective democracy.

That first reservation about the committees' performance is linked to the second: the reluctance to look at very broad issues of philosophy, principle or cultural purpose. It is, in fact, doubt-ful if parliamentary inquiries could ever deal with this kind of thing. Politicians are bound to be mainly concerned with the immediate, and the long term for them is bound to be anything beyond the next election. That is not a cynical point, and it is cer-tainly not a point specifically about Scotland: it merely indicates something about the nature of democratic politics in general. The truly great politicians are aware of this limitation, and try to sponsor other ways of linking the everyday troubles of mundane politics to the big public issues that characterise an entire era, or an entire culture. As we saw in Chapter 2, one of the ways traditionally in which politicians brought these big questions to bear on education was through the appointment periodically of national advisory committees, a practice that was abandoned in the early 1960s. Another and much more recent example, but not in education, was the report that led to the Constitutional Convention in 1989, and hence to the Scottish parliament: the Claim of Right of 1988, which was produced by people who could step back from politics and look at Scotland's constitutional status in the context of the broad sweep of history. One question for the future is how this kind of vision can be brought back into Scotland's democratic processes while continuing to respect the inescapable demands of the here and now. That, too, is a question for the last two chapters.

CHAPTER 7

Educational Lessons

The controversies about Higher Still were never only about data management. Whether or not the head of the inspectorate was correct to claim that everything was going well until the first candidates had sat their exams in May 2000, there ought to be no denying the very bitter divisions over educational philosophy and cultural purpose which the reforms provoked during the six years after their announcement in 1994. This book has not been only about what happened in 2000; it has also been about what an examination system is for. There was agreement by 1994 that reform was needed, although there was no agreement on what kind, despite subsequent claims that there was. The reason it was possible to believe this is because there seemed to be no alternative: Higher Still was announced and that seemed to be that. Most educationalists simply acquiesced. During the ensuing six years, there was no wide-ranging discussion of how an examination system that had been designed for an academic minority could be made consistent with Scotland's relatively successful comprehensive schools, while also retaining the intellectual integrity on which its reputation had rested. Perhaps now, belatedly, that discussion can take place properly. So the lessons that are sketched in this chapter deal with both the immediate administrative matters and the much broader questions as well.

ADMINISTRATION

The most pressing matter is obviously to get things working for year 2001, and to persuade people that the system is credible. This will not be easy, since several new aspects of the reform are happening for the first time in 2001, notably the Advanced Higher. No doubt much of the detailed management work is already being done, and presumably the data management, at least, will be carried out correctly. That was the inescapable recommendation of the report from the management consultants Deloitte and Touche. These things just have to be assumed because the SQA has still not deigned to tell us exactly what went wrong. Even Deloitte and Touche has admitted to not having full information on what was required to sort out all the problems. The SQA has issued bland lists of defects described in very general terms, but it has not provided the kind of technical account that would allow experts in information technology or in management-information systems to judge what had gone wrong and whether the SQA understands how to put it right. Despite everything, it still expects us to trust it.

Whatever these still inscrutable technicalities may be, three things can be said with some confidence. The first is that any exam system depends on trust. Students and teachers have to trust that the exam will fairly reflect the syllabus. They and the SQA have to trust markers to do their job well. Everyone has to trust the SQA to oversee all this, to put in place the appropriate procedures for quality control and to apply rigorous analysis to each year's results so that lessons for improving the systems can be learned for subsequent years. On the whole, the old Examination Board did all this, or at least was believed to do it. This widespread belief has helped to ensure that Scotland has never had the crisis of confidence in examination standards that afflicts England every year.

But confidence has obviously been shattered now, and will take many years to restore. The SQA needs to demonstrate, in public, that it has proper quality-control procedures in place. At least a large segment of that public will be sceptical, students and teachers above all. The procedures must include such matters as the moderation of any internal assessment that continues (a point to which we return later), the vetting of the standard of the exam papers, the recruitment and training of markers, the transfer of data from markers to the SQA computers, the reconciling of exam results with what schools have been expecting of their students, the issuing of certificates and the administration of appeals. No doubt there are other things too: the main point is that there is a great deal, and that the SQA still has been reluctant to tell us what it intends to do to reassure us.

The second point on administration is that the only really thorough system of quality control is one that is decentralised. The chief executive of the Scottish Higher Education Funding Council put this rather well on 29 September 2000 before the Lifelong Learning committee, describing the culture he tried to establish in his own organisation: 'We do not have a culture of blame. People recognise that things slip up at times and feel that they can bring such matters to the attention of the next layer of the organisation without being held to account in a way that is threatening to them.'

In the context of the schools exams, that obviously must apply to the SQA's own staff who, as the Deloitte and Touche inquiry discovered, were aware of the emerging problems but were ignored by their senior managers. But for Higher Still as a whole, it must apply throughout the education system. Teachers, students and, where appropriate, their parents must be given a more formal role in detecting failures in quality, in reporting them, and in having their concerns treated seriously, not merely 'noted' by ad hoc committees that have no power in this regard, such as the Higher Still Liaison Group. The old subject panels of the Examination Board were part of that, allowing the teachers on them to monitor standards, but even at the best of times they met relatively infrequently. What is also needed is an efficient system by which the concerns of teachers and others can be relayed back to people who can take decisions quickly. To encourage teachers to do this, they have to be persuaded that it is worth doing, and so there have to be mechanisms by which they actually have a right to be heard.

But the third point is that all this comes at a price. If it is not to add to the stress that teachers and students already face, then it has to be paid for. For example, teachers cannot be expected to take on an extra quality-control function on top of their already onerous workload. The same applies to one of the dafter suggestions to have emerged – that all teachers be contractually obliged to do some SQA marking. You will get the best advice from teachers, and the best marking, only if it is a voluntary activity, because then, on the whole, the teachers who come forward to do it will be those who are most skilled in relevant ways. But to allow them to come forward they must have time, which means paying for extra staff in schools. That is a political issue, made all the more sensitive by the parallel and wider concerns about teachers' pay and working conditions.

CREDIBILITY

The credibility of the Scottish exam system is partly, again, a matter of trust. But how to establish trust is not in fact clear. On the one hand, it is generally assumed that public transparency is likely to enhance trust. In the present context, that has underlain the suggestion that marked exam scripts should be made available to students, to reassure people that the marking is fair, and to allow teachers to help future students to perform well. But one academic authority on examination systems internationally, Professor Alison Wolf of the Institute of Education in London, has noted this paradox: 'Transparency and public confidence are by no means positively correlated. In countries where the assessment process is left very much to the teachers and educational professionals, there appears to be less, not more, anxiety about standards.'

Professor Wolf acknowledges that openness might be a response to distrust rather than a cause of it, but goes on: 'Given the inherently imperfect and non-mechanical nature of assessment judgements, one may doubt that further auditing and oversight will increase confidence, and predict that it is more likely to decrease it further.'

Nevertheless, what has not diminished in Scotland is the generally high level of trust in teachers. That was already high before the crisis in 2000: in a survey for the Organisation for Economic Co-operation and Development in 1996, 63 per cent of Scots said that teachers were well respected, better than in almost all other OECD countries. This standing has almost certainly risen as a result of the present crisis, since the one thing that everyone seems to agree on is that teachers taught the courses, issued the warnings, and were ignored. So although Professor Wolf may be correct that excessive amounts of audit actually may diminish public confidence, turning more of the responsibility for quality control over specifically to teachers in Scotland may enhance it.

But one thing can be said with some certainty: everyone will be alert to an unprecedented extent in summer 2001. Every single candidate will be a test of the exam system's credibility, and teachers will inspect very closely whether their students' results are plausible compared with how they have been performing throughout their years in school. Inexplicable discrepancies will be well publicised, and the SQA will have to have its defences intact. It will have to have answers to the questions that will come again about data management, the administration of marking and the automatic checking of candidates' performance in the external exam compared to their school work. And these answers will have to be persuasive to a public which, because of the events of 2000, is better educated than ever before about how the exam system operates and where it can go wrong.

In any case, credibility is not only about quality control. It is also about assessment philosophy. We saw in Chapter 3 that there has been a shift away from so-called 'norm-referencing', by which the results of each individual student depend on the performance of all the other students in the same diet of exams. But making the leap from that to 'competence-based assessment' is fraught with difficulties. It may be perfectly acceptable educationally to agree that assessment should be 'criterion-referenced' – that students should be judged on what they can, and cannot, do, and on what they do, and do not, know. But to describe this as being only about 'competence' is a fallacious importing into education of some of the necessary technical skills that make up part of vocational education (but only part even of that). The whole Higher Still structure of multiple unit assessments seems to be a drift towards the idea that you can subdivide fields of knowledge into discrete units of competence, which may be assessed separately. Some knowledge can be tested like that – even some knowledge that is relevant to academic work (such as some of the manipulative skills of algebra). But not all of it can, and indeed it is plausible to argue that the most important aspects of learning cannot be reduced at all to small chunks, separately assessed.

Part of the purpose of an education system is passing on a society's culture, and equipping students to criticise as well as understand that culture. But that means dealing with the culture as a whole, or at least dealing with individual aspects as a whole (such as literature, science, the workings of society itself). The reduction in length of the final external exams, the splitting of the courses into individual units, the partial replacement of goals such as the development of understanding with measures of technical competence: these tend to demean the broad cultural purpose of education. It is in precisely such circumstances that anxieties about standards really do grow, not necessarily because people doubt the systems of quality control, but because they question whether students are being given worthwhile things to learn.

THE PHILOSOPHY OF HIGHER STILL

It is in the light of considerations such as these that the philosophy of Higher Still needs to be judged. There was indeed an agreement in 1994 that some kind of change was required. But that did not amount to agreement on anything more, and certainly did not produce a coherent assessment philosophy as the basis of a way forward. In the first place, awkwardly on the table but ignored, was the case that had been made by Professor Andrew McPherson. Despite what was sometimes alleged by his critics, this was not a claim that nothing had to change. His point was, more subtly, that change was built into the existing system – that by slow, incremental adjustments, the combination of Highers and National Certificate modules was responding to student needs. We saw in Chapter 3 that, during the years following Howie's report, that system did indeed adapt in the manner which Professor McPherson predicted: his critics, including those of us who were inclined to be somewhat sceptical at the time, were proved wrong.

To have left things like that would not have been entirely satisfactory, because the philosophy of the modules was already being questioned. Scottish education has never given serious and sustained attention to vocational philosophy – to the principles that ought to underlie that part of education which is direct preparation for work. That was needed in 1992. We might have got it from a determined effort to implement Howie's scheme, because to make the Scotcert work would have required a lot more attention to its distinctive philosophy than anything which a modular scheme requires. But what is certain is that we did not get it with Higher Still. It has merely been asserted in the last six years that unifying academic and vocational education is desirable. It may be, but we won't know until we ask what each of these is separately.

THE SOCIAL STANDING OF SCOTTISH EXAMINATIONS

In some important respects, Scottish *education* was not affected in the year 2000: the problem was in assessment. It is true that the modularisation of courses must have changed the character of teaching and learning, but for the time being there were the same teachers, and broadly the same kinds of students, as there have been for several years. Teachers came out of the whole debacle well, although their wider concerns about the underlying philosophy of Higher Still are still not being addressed. Teachers are generally trusted, and faith in the comprehensive system of secondary schools remains high. There is also enthusiasm for the current expansion of higher education, encouraging which is one of the main purposes of the Higher Still reforms: in the 1999 Scottish Social Attitudes Survey, only 2 per cent felt that the expansion had gone too far, and fully 50 per cent wanted it to go further.

Nevertheless, the standing of the examinations having collapsed, who knows what the long-term consequences will be? There seems little doubt that, unless the problems can be fully sorted out by the summer of 2001 – an almost impossible task – some schools will move in despair to using the English A-levels, especially now that some of the worst features of these are being mitigated by the option of taking a broader range of subjects rather than specialising prematurely. A more radical option would be to adopt the International Baccalaureate, which had its origins in the 1960s in an attempt to provide a common programme for the various international schools that were being developed around the world. International schools tend to teach students from a very broad range of national backgrounds, usually the children of diplomats and such like. The International Baccalaureate is now offered in over 500 schools in more than 70 countries to 21,000 students, and is accepted by about 700 universities as a valid entrance qualifications. It is provided at two levels − higher and subsidiary − over two years, and there is a requirement to combine breadth and depth, and to study an aspect of philosophy. All candidates have to show that they have developed an international understanding. A study of it in the journal *Educational Studies* in 1997 by Mary Hayden and Cynthia Wong at Bath University (from where these statistics come) concluded that it was 'successful internationally in providing a broad and rigorous academic programme which facilitates international mobility'. It is, however, aimed at students who would be among the most academically able. The Howie committee − as we noted in Chapter 3 − also praised the programme, but concluded that 'under current conditions only a relatively small proportion of fifth- and sixth-year students could aspire to successful attainment'.

Individual independent schools could choose such different examination systems on their own initiative, although the upheaval involved would tend to make them cautious in doing so. Public-sector schools would have to wait for a decision by their local authority, but that may come. One early signal was the decision in autumn 2000 by Highland Council to withhold part of their fee from the SQA until they had evidence that the authority could do its job. If the users of exams are to be treated as 'customers', in the language of the SQA interim chief executive, they have to be expected to take their business elsewhere when they do not get the service they have paid for.

THE ROLE OF EXAMINATIONS

Standing back from the particular controversies over this specific reform, we can see also that it raises some deep questions about the educational and social purposes of examinations. The recent reforms have been the culmination of over a century of ever-expanding assessment, creating an education system that is increasingly meritocratic in the sense of being based more and more on certification. In some respects, the downfall of Higher Still assessment in the year 2000 was caused by its aspiration to assess everyone, and it was proven to be technically wanting. Debating the problems of particular technical ways of managing a burgeoning régime of assessment ignores the more fundamental question: why do we need this at all?

On the one hand, as we saw in Chapter 2, exams can be emancipating. Providing wider and wider access to public exams has been the main means by which equal opportunities were expanded during the twentieth century. Exams allowed working-class children, girls, children from ethnic minorities and Catholic children to demonstrate their true capacities in a much fairer way than in the days when selection for jobs was more strongly influenced by inherited social status than by achievement – by what sociologists have called selection by invidious ascription. Merito-cracy may be too competitive, but it's the least unfair system of selection that has yet been invented. In the words of John Gold-thorpe, professor of sociology at Oxford University: 'Questioning [meritocracy] would seem to leave the way open for a return to ascriptive criteria or, worse, to all manner of discriminatory practices in education and employment alike. Meritocracy might thus be regarded as a "necessary myth".'

On the other hand, questioning the dominance of exams is not the same as wanting to abandon them. The report of the commit-tee chaired by Professor Howie was at least aware of the implica-tions of this. As we saw in Chapter 3, it rejected modularisation mainly on the grounds that it would lead to 'over-assessment and assessment-driven learning', but it certainly did not propose to end examination altogether. Other education systems manage to run respected secondary-school systems that are not dominated by examinations to nearly the same extent that Scotland's is, and yet do test their students when appropriate. The best-known example is Sweden. As Professor Wolf notes in the chapter mentioned above, it has no examination board, no public examinations and no widely used standardised tests. Admission to the senior years of secondary school, and to university, is determined on the basis of tests administered and marked by students' own teachers. Teachers' assessment standards are checked by requiring them periodically to give standardised tests to all their students. In Professor Wolf's words: 'The tests are written by university-based groups in education faculties, who draw on the national curriculum and their own experience to prepare the items. They are taken by all students, and are used by teachers to standardise their own marks. However, they do not overrule them.'

In other words, what works today in Sweden is rather like the system that was proposed for Scotland by the 1947 Advisory Council's report on secondary education (which we reviewed in Chapter 2). Alison Wolf concludes: 'The remarkable aspect of the Swedish approach is the way it lodges final judgements with teachers, as those best placed to know a pupil's performance; but uses testing not to replace but to improve that judgement.'

The Swedish case is worth considering, not because it offers an off-the-shelf option for Scotland, but because it shows that it is possible to run a modern education system without the heavy reliance on external assessment that Scottish schools have. What is more, Sweden manages to do that without compromising equal opportunities, without returning to the invidious ascription of which Goldthorpe warns: it has one of the fairest educational and social systems in the world.

The practicability of the same approach is shown also by what happens routinely in universities in the UK. If university lecturers can be trusted to set and mark exams for their own students, with standards maintained by having their work checked by external examiners and by periodic visits from the Funding Council's quality-control committees, there is no reason why, in principle, the same could not happen in schools. Some of Higher Still's critics have inferred from the massive over-examination entailed by the unit assessments that no test done by teachers of their own students could possibly meet the needs of a fair education system. That may confuse two things: the excessive amount of assessment which Higher Still has imposed, and the question of who does it.

If – despite the Swedish and university examples – concerns are still raised about standards in a system less dominated by external exams, the most obvious reply is that the enormous amounts of assessment entailed in Higher Still have not reassured people about standards either. No one would believe assurances about standards issued by the SQA at the moment. It is not the externality of the assessment that guarantees standards, but the processes by which whoever does the setting and marking of an exam is trained and monitored. Again it comes back to a question of trust. Ultimately the most effective system of monitoring is that done by a teacher of his or her own work. You can check an individual's marking standards by sampling their work, as happens in the universities, and by then proving feedback to them on how lenient or severe they are being. But you do not need to examine every student half a dozen times per year in each subject to achieve that.

In particular, for the half of students wanting to proceed to higher education, all that is needed is a reasonably accurate measure that provides a fair prediction of whether they are likely to be able to benefit from doing so. After all, the correlation between students' exam performance at school and their eventual results at university is relatively weak: in technical terms, about two thirds of the variation in student performance at the end of first year cannot be explained by the variation in their entry qualifications. We will, in fact, have a test of that in three or four years' time when the students who entered in autumn 2000 graduate. In some universities, notably Aberdeen, Napier, Stirling and Paisley, some of them will have been admitted on the basis of teachers' predictions of their grades. It will be interesting to monitor whether they perform any differently from their peers who were admitted on the basis of full exam certificates. If the results are much the same, we have to ask whether going to all the bother of examining everyone in minute detail by means of external exams is really the most satisfactory way of selecting students for university.

That point is, in fact, just one instance of a more general one.

There is no need for external testing at any point in a student's career other than the final one. In Denmark there are more external exams than in Sweden, but only at the leaving point. Before that, students are assessed by their own teachers. It has already been suggested in Scotland that Standard Grade need no longer be an external exam for the vast majority of students who stay on at school beyond age 16. The same ought to be true of standardised testing in primaries and early secondaries. What matters to each student is their endpoint, not how they got there.

For example, Scotland gets terribly anguished about comparisons of performance with other countries that tend to show some (though not all) aspects of numeracy being no better than average at ages 9–13. But Scotland also has the highest rate of successful completion of higher education in Europe, and performance in the Higher Grade exams (before 2000) was also notably high by international standards. If we are letting young people develop at their own pace to a greater extent than some countries which force them to achieve rigid age-related outcomes, then maybe we are doing something quite humane and ultimately more effective educationally. And if that is so, perhaps we should do more of it – adopt the philosophy that (in the words of that 1947 Report again) the years of youth should be filled with 'security, graciousness and ordered freedom' – not anarchy, but freedom within much broader constraints than we currently impose. Testing, age-related criteria and public anguish over 'standards' that are separately measured all the way through a student's time at school are not consistent with that.

EDUCATIONAL PHILOSOPHY

As well as Higher Still being the latest episode in the growth of assessment, it is also the most recent instance of expansion being driven by technocratic considerations. The educational question of why education should expand is rarely asked.

It is true that one debate which does appear to be taking place is about education's role in the economy. Providing uninterrupted supplies of skilled labour is the justification of expansion that is most often heard. In actual fact, despite the political consensus on this, there is little hard evidence that higher overall levels of education and training really are the cause of more rapid economic growth. The crude links that can be found between educational levels and growth are usually only correlations and not causations: statistical associations that turn out to be explained away when other factors are taken into account. The main reason for this has to do with a question about whether education is a cause or an effect of national economic success. Rich countries tend to spend more on education and training than poor countries for essentially social reasons. People want education to get jobs for themselves or their children, and for cultural reasons, and so in a democracy more education is frequently one of the first priorities for new public and private spending. So, simply noting that rich countries have more effective education systems proves nothing. Providing job opportunities for educationally successful individuals is not equivalent to raising the overall growth rate of the economy. Education helps to influence which people get the jobs available, but does not necessarily determine how many jobs there are overall.

For those who accept that education ought to expand, the most usual non-economic argument is on the grounds of promoting equal opportunities, but even here the question of opportunity to do what is rarely mentioned. This gets us back to the questions about the purpose of an examination system. Assessment for all, providing 'opportunity for all', is vacuous in itself. Nevertheless, in the absence of explicit debate about purpose, sometimes the answer is given implicitly by the conservatism of what appears to be a radical extension of equal opportunities, so that the opportunities are actually being given to something very old indeed. It is plausible to argue, for example, that one reason why Scottish comprehensive schools are relatively popular is that they were relatively conservative. They did not overthrow a century of academic education, and the main measure of their success has been in the access which they have provided to the old style of Higher Grade examination. That this was possible without causing a crisis in standards tends to show that providing certificates of some sort for all students is not worthless, provided these

certificates are differentiated by level. Saying that certificates are
available to all is not tantamount to saying that all shall have
prizes (the typical derogatory comment of critics of comprehensives in England). Standard Grade shows that. The academic
demands of the Credit awards, especially level 1, are higher than
anything available under the old O-grade, even while Standard
Grade is also providing certificates for people who would have
achieved nothing in O-grade. But for this argument to make sense,
there has to be this differentiation. It has to be accepted that the
old academic standards are being maintained at some level of the
new certificate even while extra levels are being added on below.
It is precisely this continuity that many critics of Higher Still fear
is lacking.

But even with that justification – that old standards are
embodied in the new structures – there is still an absence of
deeper questions about the purpose of education. We hear almost
nothing about its cultural purposes. And yet we don't have to go
far back in Scotland to find such purposes being to the fore in
reform. The 1977 Munn report on the curriculum for ages 14–16
offered this: 'Schools exist in and for a given society, and one of
the main functions of schooling is to equip young people with the
skills, the knowledge, and the social and moral attitudes which
will fit them for full membership of the adult community.' That
may not command universal assent, but at least it addresses
cultural matters that Higher Still simply ignores.

And then, beyond that, we seem to have lost entirely the
argument which says that education is not for anything at all: it is
for its own sake. Despite Scotland's reputation for applied knowledge – all those engineers and doctors – this is also strong in our
traditions. The most distinguished exponent of it in the last fifty
years has been Professor John Anderson, of Scottish origins and
education although ultimately based in Australia. He argued in
Education and Enquiry that education is its own goal, and that we
need to turn the question of purposes round: the purpose of life, he
said, is to lead an educated existence. That philosophy has not
usually animated mainstream education, but Scotland has also
produced a fair measure of educational dissidents who would have

subscribed to Anderson's ideas, most famously A.S. Neill in the first couple of decades of the twentieth century, but also William Boyd of Glasgow University in the 1930s, and the headteacher R.F. Mackenzie, who wrote in *A Question of Living* in 1963 that Scottish education has placed 'excessive emphasis upon the results of written examinations and has produced a class of people who combine an astonishing verbal facility with a meagre equipment of wisdom and little understanding of the complicated human situation and values involved in the words they so glibly use'.

This is not the place to analyse all the philosophical ramifications. Going back to the questions that ought to be asked about Higher Still, my own inclination is to say that there is no coherent distinction between academic and vocational education, but on the other hand I would also insist then that the best vocational preparation requires a sound academic education as its foundation. That was the old Scottish educational philosophy that dominated the universities in the nineteenth century. That's why breadth is valued in this tradition, not for its own sake, but because it acquaints us with the several purposes of human practical activity, and underpins a common human culture – a common curriculum. But philosophy is also necessary because it equips us with the intellectual tools to understand what human beings have in common. We don't have to call it philosophy, of course. It can be, in current parlance, thinking skills, praised by Professor John Nisbet of Aberdeen University for the breadth of intellect that they can encourage: 'A "thinking curriculum" is one which involves learners actively in thinking, which abhors "inert ideas" and which aims to foster transferable thinking skills.' Some of the most interesting discussions about citizenship education in Scotland at the moment do engage with these ideas, but the core of educational debate does not.

Whatever the merits of one set of ideas, the main point, however, is not that. What is needed is a wide debate about the purposes of our educational institutions and about the kinds of human being they are moulding. We have that debate in Scotland only sporadically. We have had nothing of it during the development of Higher Still.

CHAPTER 8

Political Lessons

The events of August 2000 also provoked an unprecedented debate about the way in which Scottish education is governed, and the way in which policy for it is made. Discontent that had been simmering away in specialist educational circles burst out into the open. One reason it did so was the mere existence of the Scottish parliament: the parliamentary inquiries provoked people into asking questions. If the parliament had not been there, the rhetorical conclusion to which most of this debate would have come would have been that everything would be rosy if only Scotland had the democratic accountability that would surely come with self-government. That kind of explanation has not been available since 1999, and so critics of existing structures have had to think more carefully about what consensus, accountability and open government mean in practice.

THE LEADERSHIP CLASS

Never before has Professor Walter Humes' term seemed so apt. Whatever may be said for the more benign description of Scottish policy-making as being shaped by a policy 'community', the centrally driven character of the Higher Still reforms seems to demand the much tighter description of a policy that was devised and implemented by people who were accustomed to exercising a leadership that was never seriously challenged.

The inspectorate, above all, has been in charge of the policy throughout. Its head, Douglas Osler, may quibble at the word 'policy', but the inspectors instigated and oversaw the Howie inquiry, proposed the Higher Still reform, managed its implementation and saw it as their duty to try to avert disaster when it began to threaten during 1999–2000. The details of the examinations and courses were devised by the Higher Still Development

Unit which the inspectorate set up, line managed (to use Mr Osler's own term) and monitored. The 1996 Act which set up the Scottish Qualifications Authority sanctioned the inspectors' close involvement with that body, too, just as they had been closely linked to the old Examination Board. It is hardly surprising that the inspectorate was enthusiastic about a reform that it had done so much to bring about, in some respects (in relation to school sixth year) dating right back to the 1940s. It would have taken all the credit if everything had gone well.

The inspectors' responsibility is evident, as was their unwillingness to hear contrary views. They reported in February 2000 that the implementation of Higher Still was raising no serious problems, even while schools were becoming increasingly frustrated in their attempts to process data for the SQA. When they were warned, by schools and others, that these data problems could lead to catastrophe, the inspectorate repeatedly accepted reassurances from the SQA senior management that everything would be fine. Right through the summer of 2000, as it began to intervene more urgently in the SQA's affairs, the inspectorate remained publicly silent about the problems. It may even have kept the minister uninformed too. And in the early days of the crisis in August 2000 it was presumably behind the repeated assurances which the minister made in public that matters were in hand, and would not turn out to be too serious.

The inspectorate's reaction to this kind of point in the past, from different critics on other occasions, is to dismiss the accuser as an eccentric outsider, embittered by, say, a failure to receive research funding from it, or by failure to be appointed by it to powerful positions on educational quangos. A series of critics over the years has retreated into isolation, unable to counter the sheer power over information about Scottish education which the inspectorate commands, and unable to cast any more than the occasional glint of light on how it does influence policy. No doubt that will happen – it is already happening – again now, but ridiculing or denigrating one critic will not work any more. The difference is the presence of the parliament. The focus made available by the Education committee's inquiry has allowed concerted criticism of the inspectorate to be made by a great variety of bodies, with no collusion at all. The members of the committee themselves were frustrated by what they perceived to be the lack of candour coming from Mr Osler. That is why they asked him back to appear on his own, and even then they were not satisfied.

The point that has probably been most telling in this connection has been that warnings were given, and were ignored – not just the specific warnings about data management, but also the deeper concerns about other aspects of Higher Still, or even about the reform as a whole. When that history has been presented in public before the inquiry, the reaction by people outwith the education system – including by MSPs themselves – has been dismay. So the case now being made against the inspectorate is being subsumed into a much more general case against Scotland's civic establishment. The theme in the campaigns for home rule which said that Scotland needed a parliament to rid its civic life of complacency has not gone away. Events such as the collapse of Higher Still will, if anything, have given it new cogency. How on earth could something so important to so many young people have been managed so badly? That may be unfair – maybe a more open form of government would not have prevented it – but the accusation is made against a body, the inspectorate, whose entire style is based on an aura of authority. If it really is in charge, why did it not get it right?

EDUCATIONAL POLICY-MAKING

One lesson that is likely to be learned is that massive consultation is not the same as making policy by thorough consensus. The consultation which the Howie committee undertook was genuinely wide-ranging, anticipating by a decade some of the principles that the Scottish parliament has been trying to adopt. As with Andrew Cubie's report on student finance in 1999, this was aided by the style of the convener. Professor Howie and Mr Cubie did not pretend that they knew the answers in advance, and they received candid responses as a result.

The difference lay in what then emerged. Professor Howie chose to respect the consensus so far as criticism of the existing system was concerned, but to ignore it on what needed to be done. Mr Cubie didn't, and had his recommendations adopted by a new consensus (even though only partly by the Scottish government). The consultation on Professor Howie's proposals – overseen by the inspectorate – was also thorough, and ensured that they never really stood much chance of being accepted. Maybe that is what the inspectorate knew would happen, leaving the way open for its own long-standing preferred option of a suite of two-year courses in fifth and sixth year. We will not know until the official papers are released. But what can be said is that the consensus against the status quo and against tracking left the inspectorate with a clear field for its own proposals.

But that is where the consultation really began to wither. Where exactly did the original Higher Still proposals of 1994 come from? Not from Howie: he had explicitly ruled out both modularisation and the two-year option. Not from the pre-Howie consensus: very few people recommended anything resembling Higher Still, preferring to leave the Highers as they were and to develop the National Certificate modules. And not from the consultation on Howie: many submissions did, by then, suggest modularisation, but few suggested anything like the Advanced Higher, and none would have contemplated the sheer scale of the internal assessment that emerged. It did not come from the political parties either: as we have seen, they took little interest until the summer of 2000. So the answer has to be that Higher Still was the product mainly of thinking within the inspectorate itself, expediently plucking morsels from the consultation process and from Howie's report, but sticking them together in its own style.

Whatever the truth of that, it is certain that there was hardly any fully public discussion of the details of implementation thereafter. There was discussion in the specialist committees, but these took place in private. In due course there was discussion at the training sessions for principal teachers, but they had no authority to make changes. The best they could hope for was that the Higher Still Development Unit and the inspector who was always present would voluntarily act on their suggestions. The impression which teachers had was that they rarely did.

This area of implementing reforms in public policy is where the greatest need for political change lies. The Scottish parliament is beginning to make a big impact on how policy is made preceding legislation. It is also beginning to open up the workings of the civil service and the quangos, and the Higher Still inquiries are the latest and most sustained in a series of such investigations (others include Scottish Opera, the Scottish Tourist Board and the role of Local Enterprise Companies). But it has not yet turned its attention to the ways in which policy is implemented, and yet the character of a policy can be shaped by that as much as by legislation.

We don't have ready-made models for how to conduct an open process of implementation, but to see the problems, consider in more detail the role of the teacher unions in the Higher Still Liaison Group from late 1998 onwards. On the face of it, this was a model of representative decision-making: the Group embraced teachers, parents' leaders and local authorities as well as the inspectorate and the Scottish Office. But even putting matters like that is to attribute too much benignity to the inspectorate: it set up the Group only after teachers had voted overwhelmingly to boycott the reform. Ordinary teachers were not consulted in advance on whether taking part in such a group would allay the concerns they were expressing through that vote. They may subsequently have accepted the compromise, but through force of circumstance as much as anything else, and the vote at their conference six months later to abandon all unit assessments suggests that even that acceptance was very grudging indeed.

This is not to impugn the motives of the EIS leaders who did join the group. They believed in the principles of Higher Still – and had other conference motions to back them – and, like all good union negotiators, were able to spot a compromise that would be politically acceptable to the other side. The point is simply that we do not have the policy-implementation structures by which a boycott vote such as the union members gave in November 1998 could be translated into decentralised structures of implementation in which these same members could translate their hostility into constructively achieving change. We do not have these because the true powers at the centre – in this case, the inspectorate – would never, in present circumstances, let go to that extent.

In short, implementation of policy ought to be a partnership just as much as the Consultative Steering Group has put in place for the parliament in the devising of policy. Good implementation depends on pluralism and sharing of ideas and responsibility just as much as on good legislation. So something like the CSG principles should be applied to what happens after legislation is passed, or after a major policy statement has been issued. In the making and implementing of education policy in schools the most significant relevant partners are teachers, students, parents, local authorities, the skilled personnel in the variety of quangos and the Education Department, further and higher education, and employers. It is no longer adequate to have most of these interests represented by a process of patronage – 'representatives' selected by the inspectorate itself – and for some (such as the Department) to have almost a monopoly of influence. There has to be a guaranteed and democratic representation of the different social partners on the committees that oversee policy, and a means by which their voices can be heard in public. That requires a more open culture of implementation, so that public debate can continue to take place on principles even while practice is being developed. Principles never go away: developing good practice necessarily entails discussing questions of purpose as well.

It also requires a much more open system of accountability among quangos, and here the lessons to be learned from the exams crisis and from the controversies over the development of Higher Still are very wide-ranging indeed. At board level, the SQA is not an especially undemocratic or inexpert body. The board which was in charge when the crisis broke in summer 2000 contained a range of relevant educational expertise, and it had always been required to publish the same kinds of annual reports and policy statements as most of the other committees that run Scottish public policy. The Deloitte and Touche inquiry into the exams crisis found, it is true, fairly damning evidence on the lack of adequate communication between board and management: SQA officials kept the board in the dark, and the board failed to ask sufficiently searching questions. But they would not be alone among Scottish quango authorities in that respect. Indeed, despite regularly receiving minutes of board meetings, the inspectors and civil servants in the government's Education Department saw nothing remiss in the SQA practices until well into the disastrous year 2000. What the SQA was doing was, on the whole, perfectly normal.

And that's the deeper problem. Although inducing the SQA board and its chairman to resign may have been politically necessary after the publication of the Deloitte and Touche report, it was dealing with symptoms more than causes. The problems of the SQA illustrate a wider malaise: the need for much greater public scrutiny, an expectation that the affairs of quango boards be conducted mostly in public, and a requirement that the lay board be properly and fully briefed by officials. Something of this happens in the better-run quangos, but not enough, and not so much as to amount to systematic democratisation.

Ad-hoc changes to the SQA are no more than palliatives that could make the accountability even more opaque – for example, the proposals that have been made to appoint an 'exams commissioner' in the Education Department to oversee their work, or the suggestion that the entire administration of the exam system be brought back inside the Department (where it was until 1965, and which temporarily happened after the Deloitte and Touche report appeared). Doing either of these things would solve none of the problems of accountability, and indeed would simply displace the problems onto the core civil service. In any case, as we have seen in abundant detail in earlier chapters, the inspectorate already closely monitors what goes on in the SQA, and they already 'line manage' the Higher Still Development Unit, and yet that did not prevent the disaster of 2000 coming about.

What is needed is a more fundamental change in the whole culture of quangos. In the words of the John Wheatley Centre inquiry into quangos in 1996, which was discussed in Chapter 5, 'the establishment of a Scottish parliament will give civil servants and officials an opportunity not to be hidebound by traditional outlooks'. And they concluded that 'it is important for our democracy that the operations of government are susceptible to close scrutiny by the elected representatives of the people'.

A NATIONAL EDUCATION CONVENTION?

Where the process of democratising policy-making goes next is not determined. But one thing is certain: part of the root cause of the problems with Higher Still was a lack of democracy. There appeared to be a consensus, but it turned out not to be what could be called a social consensus. At best, it was a consensus among the leaders of various segments of civil society – the leaders of teachers, of parents and of employers as well as of the relevant government departments and quangos. That kind of consensus is better than imposition, if only because it usually smooths the way to implementation. It is less disruptive than the kinds of policy-making in which Michael Forsyth engaged when he was Scottish minister of education. No one can claim that they did not have the chance to comment on Higher Still in advance, unlike, say, on Mr Forsyth's original scheme for testing primary-school children. The question is whether their comments were listened to.

In some countries, achieving this kind of élite consensus would be difficult enough, but it has rarely been a problem in Scotland. In fact, one of main fears concerning the way that the Scottish parliament is currently operating is that it is being too nice. It is inclined sometimes simply to make legitimate again that old Scottish style of policy consensus, providing new forums through which the already powerful can talk to each other. That is better than their not doing so, but it is not the most thorough opening up of decision-making that could be imagined, and it tends to have no place for the real anger which many people feel about policies that go wrong, Higher Still being a prime example.

We all now need to cast around for ideas that could help Scottish policy-making never to repeat what has happened. One instance – although only one – is the Republic of Ireland, because it has been attempting to reconstruct its processes of educational policy-making for about a decade. The most significant idea that we could adapt is of a national education convention. The starting point in Ireland was a quite critical report on Irish education in

1991 by the Organisation for Economic Co-operation and Development. The government then published a discussion paper in 1992, which set out the need for radical reform – for example, to encourage greater equity, to broaden the curriculum, to devolve administration, to modernise the education of teachers, to develop a more effective system of quality assurance, and – crucially – to put together a more accountable style of policy-making.

These proposals attracted over a thousand written responses, and were intensively debated at well-attended regional conferences. That process culminated in the National Education Convention in Dublin which ran continuously for ten days in October 1993. Represented were 42 different organisations. There were educational groups, such as the teachers' unions, directors of education and representatives of higher education. There were numerous 'social partners', such as the National Parents Council, the National Youth Council, the Council for the Status of Women, the Forum of People with Disabilities, the Irish Employers Confederation and the churches. Most remarkably of all, there were the senior officials of the national Department of Education. The minister, Niamh Breathnach, attended throughout all the plenary sessions, even those at which she was not speaking. That was a remarkable break with tradition, partly reflecting the fact that she was the first Labour politician to fill the post in the history of the Republic. The willingness of these previously cloistered policy-makers to attend was a symptom of the slow democratisation in Irish public life that was also marked by the election of Mary Robinson as President.

The details of what they talked about matter less for us here than the ways they went about it. The whole thing was characterised by dialogue. The minister, in fact, put this well. 'Participants,' she said, 'are invited to both contribute and listen.' Dialogue was about 'enriching the debate, rather than competing for attention'. And dialogue would 'enormously enhance the quality of the policy-making process'. There was general agreement that the education system was not the property of this generation alone – far less of this generation's politicians, inspectors or civil servants. Ms Breathnach summed this up: 'Let us make the concept of trusteeship central to this Convention.'

Two fundamental points about the policy process emerged from the Convention's discussions. One was about the importance of partnership while reforms are implemented. As the background paper prepared by the Convention's secretariat put it: 'The voices of those charged with the implementation of change need to be heard and heeded' – for example, teachers, students and parents. The other lesson was that this can take a long time: 'Significant educational change is a complex task, and the time-span may be frustrating for impatient reformers.' The only way to achieve reform is by what Ms Breathnach called 'evolution, not revolution'.

These lessons have now permeated Irish education, along with the recommendations on particular areas of policy. As a result, there is a broad consensus about the way forward that more or less survived even a change of government. The policy process has been opened up, and the old leadership class – dominated by the Catholic Church – has had to cede some power. This dissemination was aided by the thorough work of the independent secretariat, headed by the distinguished historian Professor John Coolahan of Maynooth College. An important role was played by the media – not just in reporting the Convention, but also through the electronic record of the proceedings made available by RTE, the Irish broadcasting organisation.

Scotland may be able to learn from this, not by copying it exactly, but by using it as a stimulus to thinking about ways of developing a more thorough consensus than we have had. The Irish did not start in the position we are in: they used the Convention to help create a consensus. Scotland, by contrast, became used to operating by civic consensus in the 1980s when that seemed the only way to resist unwelcome reforms coming from the unpopular Conservative governments. So the question here is how to democratise the consensus, and how to ensure that it does not suffocate real, critical debate.

ARE THINGS CHANGING IN SCOTTISH POLICY-MAKING?
There are reasons to be optimistic, not through naive faith in the Scottish parliamentarians acting on their own, and not through any belief that the leadership class will change of its own volition,

but because of the very ferocity of criticism in August and September 2000. Scotland is becoming a more participative society: people are more willing to speak out, partly because of the very presence of the parliament, but partly also as a consequence of the same social processes as led to the setting up of the parliament. In common with other western countries, we have been going through a sort of participation revolution in the last few decades, and the Conservative-inspired reforms which gave parents more influence over their children's education are just as much part of that as the advent of the parliament itself. We are in an era of active citizenship.

Three features of the events of autumn 2000 stand out in this respect. The first is the bravery of teachers and headteachers in questioning the competence, and even the integrity, of some of the most senior people in Scottish education. That is a form of exemplary citizenship that is evidence of a civic culture that is no longer in awe of the venerable institutions. People are perhaps becoming more relaxed about this. If you criticised the leadership class when the Tories were in charge, you were immediately open to the accusation that there was no alternative. Any signs of disunity would risk a free-market onslaught. But that argument doesn't work any more, and so some of the instictive radicalism of Scottish society is gradually finding the confidence to express itself again.

The second is in the media. The newspapers have not always been at their best in the reporting of the parliament, but on this occasion most of them did the job they are supposed to: of airing private worries and relating these to the grand issues of the day, not cynically but in the expectation that a critical press is absolutely essential to democracy. In a more specialist way, the same was true of the *Times Educational Supplement Scotland*, and without its patient coverage of all the technical educational debates over the years the memory of all the deeper flaws in Higher Still might simply have faded. The most effective work in Summer 2000 was done by BBC Scotland, which night after night led the debate, not in the sense of shaping it, but simply by being well informed and probing. There was not a single proven challenge to the veracity of any story that they ran, a remarkable achievement given the heat of the events. The climax of their coverage was the special television debate on 22 August, which had an immediacy that would have been lacking in the old days before the parliament was set up. Of course it did not get answers, and of course it was adversarial (two of the criticisms that were mentioned afterwards privately by people in authority). But that's exactly the point. A democratic media does not have to be constructive, and certainly ought never to be deferential towards people in power. Active citizenship requires programmes like this.

And the third point is about the parliament itself. As we saw in Chapter 6, the parliamentary inquiries focused debate. That was a crucial public service. It shows that the mere presence of a parliament can, sometimes, be an achievement in itself. It can help ordinary people to feel that they are taking control of events that might otherwise induce despair or cynicism. Lessons do then have to be learnt, but the starting point is to provide a means to national catharsis. The seriousness with which the parliament (as opposed to the government) immediately took the crisis must have given a sense of legitimacy to many teachers, and a sense of hope to their students. Mary Mulligan, convener of the Education committee, was indeed brave to propose an inquiry while her ministerial colleagues were still dismissing the critics of the SQA as 'irresponsible', but her initiative was the only one consistent with a parliament that responds to people's concerns.

Having said all that, however, there are still doubts, still reasons to believe that we have a long way to go in Scotland before we have a fully participative democracy, or a fully responsive system of policy making. The media could only go part of the way to uncovering the true extent of governmental responsibility, and most of them got rather sidetracked into the specific issue of when and what the minister knew. That did matter, of course, and the refusal to accept responsibility for how policy is implemented was one of the more dismaying aspects of the evidence which Sam Galbraith gave to the parliamentary inquiry on 30 October: we won't have an open democracy until ministers are accountable for the ways in which policies have their impact.

By the time he gave evidence, Mr Galbraith had been replaced by Jack McConnell following Donald Dewar's death and the election of Henry McLeish as First Minister. Mr Galbraith took the Osler line that everything was well with Higher Still until the moment at which students had finished sitting their exams in May or June 2000. He refused to accept that there were more than 'a few pockets of discontent' about the Higher Still programme, and he rejected any notion that the minister had responsibility for the details of implementation – such as the fundamental matter of Higher Still's philosophy of assessment. Since he also agreed with Mr Osler that the inspectorate is not responsible for policy either, Mr Galbraith's evidence left us with the democratically absurd proposition that no-one at the top is responsible for the principled issues that implementation inevitably raises. The minister is not responsible, because these principles are operational matters: 'Implementation of policy,' he said to the committee, is 'for the SQA and the Higher Still Development Unit.' And the inspectorate is not responsible, because these principles are more than merely mechanical details: 'The inspectorate does not make decisions about policy.' Or, to put this contradiction starkly: the minister is not responsible for implementation because it is not policy, and the inspectorate is not responsible for implementation because it is policy.

Nevertheless, important though the political role in overseeing implementation is, it is of less long-term importance to creating an accountable system of government than the wider role of inspectors, civil servants, the SQA and the Higher Still Development Unit. It is understandable why the media focused on Mr Galbraith, whose face and role would be well-known to many readers and viewers, and the obscurity of the other personnel is partly a consequence of opaque policy-making itself. But that is a vicious circle. Until the internal workings of government are dramatised as fully as the exchanges across the floor of the parliamentary chamber, the details of how policies are implemented will never receive the democratic scrutiny that they are due. That these workings can be made interesting, even riveting, was shown by the inquiry sessions which cross-examined the head of the inspectorate and the head of the Education Department.

The parliamentary inquiries only began to indicate the general lessons that are to be drawn about the role and accountability of quangos. In their important and necessary task of investigating this specific incident, they have no more than prepared the way for a much fuller investigation of how we find the right balance in public policy between devolving responsibility to people with appropriate expertise and refusing to accord expertise undue weight. Similar questions run right through other parts of education, even those parts which are governed by quangos that seem to be above reproach. For example, the higher education funding council was rightly chosen by the Lifelong Learning committee as a model of how to run a quango accountably and efficiently, but even that body can hardly be said to be encouraging active public consideration of the meaning and purpose of a mass system of higher education. We have drifted into that, just as we have drifted into assessment for all at ages 17–18, without an examination of fundamental issues of philosophy. Maybe it is unfair to expect quangos themselves to do that – maybe they are unavoidably concerned mainly with technical matters – but then that passes responsibility back to the politicians. If the parliamentary committees, too, are not in a position to raise questions of deep purpose, perhaps we have to return to the way in which these questions were raised in our past. Old styles of advisory council would not be acceptable today: they belonged to an era of acute paternalism, and of unshaken faith in the superiority of Scottish education. That has passed. But there is no reason at all why broad advisory councils could not be appointed again, more representative than before, more willing to conduct their affairs in public, and more transparent in their relationship with the democratic process. If we can have consultative inquiries to investigate specific matters such as student finance or the reform of examinations, can we not also have them to look at what all this is for?

So maybe the way forward politically is through a combination of four things. There needs to be a series of specialist inquiries into various aspects of Scottish education, culminating in a public debate about philosophy and purpose. The response to these debates needs to be public and with wide participation, and a National Convention may be the best means of achieving that. The conclusions have to be picked up by the parliament itself – not just the government, the civil servants and the inspectors, but in the public forum of the nation's elected representatives. And there has to be sustained public participation in the implementation of every aspect of the reforms that may ensue.

That would be a lengthy process; thinking about philosophical questions always is – and politicians and the media would have to be patient. So, too, is the careful implementation of radical reforms that will actually work. But the scale of the anger and outspokenness that was shown in late summer 2000 suggests that people in Scotland would take part in these exercises with enthusiasm. Education affects us all. It is simply too valuable to be left to any single social group. It is certainly too important to be left to educational experts.

Guide to Further Reading

This guide notes the main sources on which the book has drawn, and suggests ways in which readers could follow the topics further.

CHAPTER 1

The material in this chapter is based mainly on newspaper files, BBC Scotland's website (http://www.bbc.co.uk/scotland/) and information given directly to the author by some participants in the events described. Some use has also been made of the evidence submitted to the parliamentary inquiries: see notes on Chapter 6 below.

CHAPTER 2

The definitive history of the Highers is:

Philip, H. (1992), *The Higher Tradition*, Dalkeith: Scottish Examination Board.

General histories of Scottish education since the late-nineteenth century can be found in:

Anderson, R. D. (1983), *Education and Opportunity in Victorian Scotland*, Edinburgh: Edinburgh University Press.

Gray, J., McPherson, A. and Raffe, D. (1983), *Reconstructions of Secondary Education: Theory, Myth and Practice Since the War*, London: Routledge and Kegan Paul.

McPherson, A. (1983), 'An angle on the geist: persistence and change in the Scottish educational tradition', in W.M. Humes and H.M. Paterson (eds) *Scottish Culture and Scottish Education*, Edinburgh: John Donald, 216–43.

McPherson, A. (1993), 'Schooling', in A. Dickson and J.H. Treble (eds), *People and Society in Scotland*, vol III, 1914–1990, Edinburgh: John Donald, 80–107.

The specific issues concerning the widening of access in the 1920s are analysed by:

Stocks, J. (1995), 'The people versus the department: the case of Circular 44', *Scottish Educational Review*, 27, 48–60.

Scottish educational policy making is analysed by:

Humes, W.M. (1986), *The Leadership Class in Scottish Education*, Edinburgh: John Donald.

McPherson, A. and Raab, C.D. (1988), *Governing Education*, Edinburgh: Edinburgh University Press.

The development of the National Certificate modules is described by:

Fairley, J. and Paterson, L. (1991), 'The reform of vocational education and training in Scotland', *Scottish Educational Review*, 23, 68–77.

The change from norm-referenced to criterion-referenced assessment in Scotland is discussed in several of the contributions to a book on the development of Standard Grade edited by two of Scotland's leading authorities on the curriculum:

Brown, S. and Munn, P. (eds) (1985), *The Changing Face of Education 14 to 16*, Windsor: NFER-Nelson.

More general writing on criterion-referenced and competence-based assessment is in:

Burke, J. (1989), *Competency-Based Education and Training*, London: Falmer.

Wolf, A. (1994), *Competence-Based Assessment*, Buckingham: Open University Press.

CHAPTER 3

Most of the material used in this chapter comes from unpublished submissions that were made to the Howie committee and that were subsequently made on its report, and newspaper reports of these (especially in the *Times Educational Supplement Scotland*). The Howie report is:

Scottish Office Education Department (1992), *Upper Secondary Education in Scotland*, Edinburgh: HMSO.

Some of Andrew McPherson's analysis of it is in:

McPherson, A. (1992), 'The Howie report on post-compulsory

schooling', in L. Paterson and D. McCrone (eds), *Scottish Government Yearbook*, Edinburgh: Unit for the Study of Government in Scotland, 114–30.

McPherson, A. (1992), 'Critical reflections on the Howie report', in *Critical Reflections on Curriculum Policy: the SCRE Fellowship Lectures 1992*, Edinburgh: Scottish Council for Research in Education, 29–52.

CHAPTER 4

As in Chapter 3, the material used here is mainly from unpublished submissions on Howie and on the Higher Still proposals, together with the reports of the development of Higher Still in the *Times Educational Supplement Scotland* and other newspapers. For the later stages of the development, use has also been made of the submissions to the parliamentary inquiries, the report by Deloitte and Touche for all of which evidence, (see notes on Chapter 6 below), and material provided to the author by teachers. The Higher Still proposals are in:

Scottish Office (1994), *Higher Still: Opportunity for All*, Edinburgh: Scottish Office.

The criticisms of Higher Stll computing are developed in more detail in:

Bird, D., Conlon, T. and Swanson, J. (1995), 'Computing and information technology in Higher Still: let's get it right', *Scottish Educational Review*, 28, 3–15.

The objections to Higher Still English are developed into a broad cultural critique in:

Scottish Association of Teachers of Language and Literature (1999), *Sense and Worth*, Edinburgh: SATOLL.

CHAPTER 5

The main works analysing Scottish educational policy making are noted under Chapter 2 above. Walter Humes' analysis of Michael Forsyth's tenure of the education ministry is in:

Humes, W. (1995), 'The significance of Michael Forsyth in Scottish education', *Scottish Affairs*, no. 11, spring, 112–30.

The most recent and thorough critical account of the Scottish inspectorate is in Chapter 7 of the book by McPherson and Raab referred to under the notes for Chapter 2 above. The former head of the inspectorate, Nisbet Gallacher, gave his account of its role in:

Gallacher, N. (1999), 'The Scottish inspectorate and their operations', in T.G.K. Bryce and W.M. Humes (eds), *Scottish Education*, Edinburgh: Edinburgh University Press, 136–45.

There are several other chapters in this large volume that deal with aspects of Higher Still and the exam system more generally.

The potential relationship between education and the Scottish parliament is analysed in:

Paterson, L. (2000), *Education and the Scottish Parliament*, Edinburgh: Scottish Academic Press.

The John Wheatley Centre report on quangos is:

John Wheatley Centre (1996), *Quangos: Policy Proposals for a Scottish Parliament*, Edinburgh: John Wheatley Centre [now the Centre for Scottish Public Policy].

Richard Parry's article on quangos and the Scottish parliament is:

Parry, R. (1999), 'Quangos and the structure of the public sector in Scotland', *Scottish Affairs*, no. 29, autumn, 12–27.

The accountability argument in the three decades of recent campaigning for a parliament can be traced in the speeches, pamphlets and articles collected in:

Paterson, L. (1998), *A Diverse Assembly: the Debate on a Scottish Parliament*, Edinburgh University Press.

The Consultative Steering Group report on the procedures of the parliament is:

Scottish Office (1998), *Shaping Scotland's Parliament*, Edinburgh: Stationery Office.

Two articles dealing specifically with how policy was made for Higher Still are:

Raffe, D. (1997), 'Upper-secondary education', in M. Clark and P. Munn (eds), *Education in Scotland*, London: Routledge, 67–80.

Raffe, D. and Howieson, C. (1998), 'The Higher Still policy process', *Scottish Affairs*, no. 24, summer, 90–108.

CHAPTER 6

This chapter uses the written and oral evidence given to the inquiries by the Scottish parliament's Education, Culture and Sport Committee and Enterprise and Lifelong Learning Committee. The written submissions are available at the Scottish Parliament Information Centre, George IV Bridge, Edinburgh, and most of these have now been scanned into electronic form and are available along with the Official Record of the proceedings of the inquiries at: http://www.scottish.parliament.uk. At that site, go to 'parliamentary business', then 'committees', and then to one of these two committees. Relevant evidence can also be found in the report by management consultants Deloitte and Touche which was commissioned by the Scottish government; it can be found at http://www.scotland.gov.uk/library3/education/sqar-00.asp.

CHAPTER 7

Views about Scottish attitudes towards education are in Chapter 9 of:
Paterson, L., Brown, A., Curtice, J., Hinds, K., McCrone, D., Park, A., Sproston, K. and Surridge, P. (2001), *New Scotland, New Politics?*, Edinburgh: Edinburgh University Press.

The International Baccalaureate is described by:
Hayden, M. and Wong, C. (1997), 'The International Baccalaureate: international education and cultural preservation', *Educational Studies*, 23, 349–61.

John Goldthorpe's incisive critique of meritocracy is in:
Goldthorpe, J. (1997), 'Problems of "meritocracy"', in A.H. Halsey, H. Lauder, P. Brown and A.S. Wells (eds.), *Education: Culture, Economy, Society*, Oxford: Oxford University Press, 663–82.

Alison Wolf discusses the Swedish and several other public examination systems in:
Wolf, A. (2000), 'A comparative perspective on educational standards', in H. Goldstein and A. Heath (eds), *Educational Standards*, Oxford: Oxford University Press, 9–37.
Many of the other chapters in this volume contain valuable insights into the character and social purpose of examination systems.

A recent analysis of the relationship between school-exam results and university progress is:

McPherson, A. and Robertson, C. (1994), 'Schools' effects on attainment in school and higher education', end-of-award report to the Economic and Social Research Council, available from the Centre for Educational Sociology at Edinburgh University.

John Anderson's work is in:

Anderson, J. (1980), *Education and Enquiry*, Oxford: Blackwell.

John Nisbet discusses thinking skills in:

Nisbet, J. (1993), 'The thinking curriculum', *Educational Psychology*, 13, 281–9.

The life and works of the Scottish radical educator R.F. Mackenzie are the subject of a recent biography:

Murphy, P. (1998), *The Life of R.F. Mackenzie*, Edinburgh: John Donald.

CHAPTER 8

The Irish National Education Convention is discussed by:

Gleeson, J. (1998), 'A consensus approach to policy-making: the case of the Republic of Ireland', in I. Finlay, S. Niven and S. Young (eds), *Changing Vocational Education and Training*, London: Routledge, 41–69.

Some other aspects of the impact of the Scottish parliament on Scottish governing institutions are discussed in the book by Paterson (2000) noted under Chapter 5 above, and in:

Hassan, G. and Warhurst, C. (eds) (1999), *A Different Future*, Edinburgh: Centre for Scottish Public Policy and Big Issue in Scotland.